272

Twenty-five visions

THE FUTURE OF BRANDS

Edited by Rita Clifton and Esther Maughan

MACMILLAN
Business

Interbrand

First published 2000 by
MACMILLAN PRESS LTD
Houndmills, Basingstoke, Hampshire RG21 6XS
and London
Companies and representatives throughout the world

ISBN 0–333–77673–9

A catalogue record for this book is available from the
British Library.

This book is printed on paper suitable for recycling and
made from fully managed and sustained forest sources.

10 9 8 7 6 5 4 3 2 1
09 08 07 06 05 04 03 02 01 00

Printed in Great Britain by
Jarrold Book Printing
Thetford, Norfolk

Contents

Acknowledgements

As with any book of this kind, the organisational requirement has been immense. We are grateful to our offices around the world for contributing data, ideas, people and interviews. It has been a true team effort.

We would particularly like to thank: Chuck Brymer (our worldwide CEO) for his support; Amber Collins, our London director responsible for marketing, for her insights and constant energy; Laurie Dodge from our New York office, Dr Kim from Korea, Jeremy Sampson from South Africa, Paul Parkin from San Francisco, Rob Findlay from Amsterdam, Andy Milligan from London and Fernando Gastelbondo from Colombia for their interviewing skills; Brendan McMahon from Japan for his suggestions; and Jane Reeve from Italy for attempting the impossible. We have had some exceptional design input from Dominique van Roey and Melanie Lloyd, with the help of Jeremy Scholfield and Frances Newell. Susan Cross was tireless in her search for logos.

Susannah Hart, a director at our London office, helped enormously with an experienced editing eye. I must also thank the ever-patient Sarah Longhorn, my PA, without whom any future, brands or otherwise, would be difficult to contemplate.

Quite possibly, this book would have remained a nice idea in a drawer had it not been for Caroline Wilson and Esther Maughan. Caroline is one of the most determined and persuasive people I have met. She managed to organise most of the 25 interviews and photographs, send letters and outlines all over the world, and still do a day job. Esther, a former senior consultant here and my fellow editor, has been a central force behind the months of planning, interviewing and writing.

But this book would not exist without our contributors, and *The Future of Brands* is dedicated to them. They all contributed their time and personal energy to take part in this project – and to be photographed. We are particularly indebted to Lord Puttnam, Paul Smith, Geoff Lamb of the World Bank, and Professor Steve Jones, who have been previous speakers at our seminars, and so have been doubly generous.

The publishers would like to thank all those brand-owners and their agents and associates who have supplied information and illustrations for this book. It should be noted that virtually every product or corporate name mentioned in the book is a registered trademark and virtually every logo reproduced in the book is the specific property of a company.

Rita Clifton
Chief Executive
Interbrand London
June 1999

PHOTOGRAPHER CREDITS

Etienne Bol
Karl-Heinz Kalbfell, Will Hutton, Mike Clasper, Paul Smith, Thomas Carr, Sepp Blatter, Rita Karakas, Steve Jones, Patrick Gournay, Lynne Franks, Sir Michael Perry, Sandra Dawson, David Puttnam, Gary Lyon, Deepak Chopra

Dae Hee Kang, Ran Photo
San Jin Park

René Nuijens
Jo Harlow, Marieke van der Werf

Jeremy Glynn
Graham Mackay

Leo Erazo
Jorge Cárdenas

John Crum
Lee Clow, Howard Schultz, Spike Lee, Geoff Lamb, Kyle Shannon

Introduction

ABOUT THE BOOK

This book was originally conceived to mark the 25th anniversary of Interbrand as the world's first specialist brand consultancy. Quite apart from the personal birthday celebrations, we strongly believed that there was something important to be said at this time in the history of brands and branding; most importantly, about their future.

So, rather than a nostalgic 'How brands have changed over the last 25 years', the focus of a new book would be on where brands are and where they might be going in the *next* 25 years. The year 1999, with all its 'eve of new era' connotations, made it feel like a fitting time to be doing this in a new way.

Now clearly a 25-year future is capable of boggling the mind. Many of today's leading brands did not even exist 25 years ago. Even if they existed as businesses, it was an odd person who called them brands – IBM, AT&T and Citibank, for example.

However, there are still a good number of leading brands today that were strong 25 years ago: Coca-Cola, Ford, Nescafé, Heinz, Gillette, Kodak. Was there any reason why they should not be great in another 25 years? Which trends and events might affect them – whether in government, business, science and society, or for individuals, young and old, across the world?

Having first considered the range of analytical tools that could be applied to forecast the changing value of brands over time (along the lines of *The World's Greatest Brands* studies by Interbrand), we decided that a more human and qualitative solution was the only option for this kind of long-range speculation on brand futures.

In keeping with a '25' theme, and in addition to the input of our brand consultants worldwide, we wanted to host the views of 25 very different individuals.

Considering how far and how fast the applications of branding have developed, and considering how they might develop further in the future, we wanted to reflect a broad mix in our invitations to contribute to this book.

We have obviously tried to identify people from a broad spectrum of backgrounds, interests, ages, countries of birth and responsibilities. Our coverage is by no means scientific or exhaustive, nor was it intended to be.

If there are to be questions of 'Why didn't you speak to …?', 'Why did you include …?', the answer is that we just did or did not. We asked our offices around the world to suggest people – whether famous or otherwise – whose views on the world they found interesting, and whose personal or professional views might add to the debate about the future of brands in a fresh and individual way.

We have asked our 25 interviewees to focus their thoughts on the future of society in general, as well as brands in particular. While many come from a 'professional marketing' perspective, others come at brands from the point of view of observer and real-life user. Almost all talk about their personal feelings on the issues, and we set out to make the style of the interviews as informal as possible.

What is extraordinary is how common are some of the emerging themes – not only with regard to brands, but to the hopes and fears for the next age of business and society.

Brands, and the concept of branding, have now permeated every level of society – both commercial and not-for-profit. Before considering their future, it is worth reviewing how and why this universality has come about – and what it means.

BRANDS TODAY

The changing definition of brands?

It is difficult to recall a book or presentation about brands that does not begin with a version of the inevitable 'What is a brand?' question.

If it seems odd still to ask this when the practice of branding is hundreds of years old, it becomes less surprising when we think about the extraordinary changes in its application and examples.

Twenty-five years ago, who would have imagined that utilities, football teams, charities and even governments and individuals would regularly use the 'brand' word to describe themselves or their 'products'? It would have been equally difficult to predict that service and technology-based brands would so dominate the top 10 of the world's most valuable brands league table (Figure 1).

And yet, if one accepts the definition of a brand as

a mixture of tangible and intangible attributes, symbolised in a trademark, which, if properly managed, creates influence and generates value

Figure 1	The world's most valuable brands by brand value*		
	Brand	**Brand value $USm**	**Market capitalisation of parent company $USm**
1	Coca-Cola	83,845	142,164
2	Microsoft	56,654	271,854
3	IBM	43,781	158,384
4	General Electric	33,502	327,996
5	Ford	33,197	57,387
6	Disney	32,275	52,552
7	Intel	30,021	144,060
8	McDonald's	26,231	40,862
9	AT&T	24,181	102,480
10	Marlboro	21,048	112,437
11	Nokia	20,694	46,926
12	Mercedes	17,781	48,326
13	Nescafé	17,595	77,490
14	Hewlett-Packard	17,132	54,902
15	Gillette	15,894	42,951
16	Kodak	14,830	24,754
17	Ericsson	14,766	45,739
18	Sony	14,231	28,933
19	Amex	12,550	35,459
20	Toyota	12,310	85,911
21	Heinz	11,806	18,555
22	BMW	11,281	14,662
23	Xerox	11,225	27,816
24	Honda	11,101	30,050
25	Citibank	9,147	42,030

Source: Interbrand/Citibank 1999

* Interbrand regards the brand as an intangible asset that creates an identifiable economic earnings stream. Our approach to brand valuation is based on the principle of economic use which means the value the brand adds to the underlying business. Brand value is defined as the net present value of the economic profit that the brand is expected to generate in the future.

NB Brands having to be excluded from this table include: privately held businesses, for which financial information is not publicly available (e.g. Levi's, Mars and Lego); consolidated businesses where it is not possible to separate information (e.g. CNN and Time); organisations which do not generate profits in the traditional sense (e.g. Visa, BBC, Red Cross); and organisations where it is not possible to distinguish between brand and other intangibles without detailed insider information (e.g. airlines, pharmaceuticals).

there seems little reason to change that definition. The difference is in needing to think more broadly about to whom, what and where it is applied – and the often extreme differences of mix between tangible and intangible attributes. Today, several of the most valuable brands have a tiny (or in some cases, virtually zero) tangible asset base: Amazon.com, Yahoo!, and other up-and-coming 'virtual' or Internet-based companies. Increasingly, we may be in the position of saying not just that 'a company's most valuable assets are its brands' but 'this company's *only* asset is its brand'. A long way to move indeed from the earliest days of soap bars, and from the fight to get brands officially recognised as real assets in the first place.

This development is also highly relevant for the subject of this book, and is a curtain-raiser to many of the thoughts offered by our contributors on their current understanding of 'brand'. In addition to our more formal textbook definitions, the most frequent themes to emerge are that a brand is a 'relationship', a 'reputation', a 'set of expectations', a 'promise'. The new virtual brands like Yahoo! embody this idea of *promise*. After all, what greater compliment could there be to the power of a brand promise than for it to enjoy a market value of some $33.9bn and yet to be making no profits at the moment?

New brands, old truths

But it is also interesting to consider what many of our contributors and brand consultants have to say about the future of new technology-based brands, and to look at the world's most valuable brands league table by *brand strength analysis* (Figure 2), rather than current financial brand value.

While such brands have youth, market vigour and innovation on their side, they may have much to learn from the league table stalwarts about building brands that will *endure* into the next age – to provide security of earnings for their owners, and more secure employment for their people. New brand categories provide no refuge from old truths about what builds strong brands in the first place – even if they do show up in very different forms.

There are many characteristics shared by the strongest brands today, the most critical of which are: *clarity*, *consistency* and *leadership*.

- *Clarity* – of vision, mission and values, which are understood, lived and even loved by the people who need to deliver them. Clarity of what makes those values distinctive and relevant; and clarity of their ownership in both people's minds and trademark law around the world.

Figure 2	**The world's most valuable brands by brand strength***		
1	Coca-Cola	16	Heineken
2	Microsoft	17	VW
3	Gillette	18	Pepsi-Cola
4	Disney	19	Ford
5	Nescafé	20	Chanel
6	Colgate	21	General Electric
7	McDonald's	22	Kodak
8	Mercedes	23	Amex
9	Pampers	24	Nike
10	IBM	25	Bacardi
11	Sony	26	Smirnoff
12	Heinz	27	AT&T
13	Intel	28	Kelloggs
14	Marlboro	29	Barbie
15	BMW	30	Moët & Chandon

Source: Interbrand

* Interbrand's proprietary brand strength analysis determines the confidence and risk profile for a brand's earnings forecast. It is based on seven core attributes, and has been validated in more than 2,500 studies worldwide. Attributes are: market stability, leadership, trend, support, geography and protection. For further reading see Interbrand's Brand Valuation publications.

- *Consistency* – Not the old-fashioned consistency of simple product, and not to be confused with predictability. Strong brands show consistency in *who they are*, whatever they're doing; there is little long-term value in a relationship with someone who may seem to be a trusted friend one day, and an axe-murderer the next. Brands also need consistency and alignment of values in all their manifestations – whether in product, in store environment, in the way people answer the 'phone, in social responsibility. And, of course, consistency of investment.

- *Leadership* – Out of some 2,500 Interbrand studies in brand valuation throughout the world, the most discriminating factor in generating long-term brand value at the highest level is leadership. This is a brand's ability to lead and exceed expectations, to take people into new territories and new areas of product, service and even social philosophy at the right time. It is also a brand's ability to be restless about self-renewal.

New brand relationships

Looking at these criteria, it is perhaps easy to see why there is a discrepancy between the listings for brand value and brand strength.

The highest level discrepancy in ranking is for Gillette. This is not altogether surprising; while its sectors are not so explosive in today's financial terms, or as prone to speculation as new technology-based brands, Gillette has been remarkably successful at managing the brand for long-term strength. It is *clear* in positioning and values, *consistent* in brand presentation and personality, and *leads* technology and customer understanding in its sector. It is a brand constantly refreshed by new products and new consumer trends and insights.

IBM and Hewlett-Packard are obviously longer-established technology-based brands, which have demonstrated (or recovered) clarity, consistency and leadership over time. However, while the fast-growing telecommunications sector has proved profitable for Nokia and Ericsson, this is not yet reflected in confidence about the latter brands' long-term brand strength.

It is still early days, but Microsoft is a fascinating example of a 'new' brand which rides high in both tables. What the brand has perhaps lacked in consistent emotional and human values has been more than compensated for by the *clear vision* of Bill Gates and the *leadership* he has demonstrated in bringing computer power to all. Intel has also enjoyed *clarity* (as an 'enabling ingredient') and *consistency* (captured by its distinctive trademarked sound).

One of the interesting challenges for all these 'new' brands, as much as for any product brands in the past, will be how to intensify their relationships with their consumers – particularly if and when their technical product prowess becomes commonplace in people's lives.

For instance, what will happen when a 'loved' service or corporate brand enters these markets? In fact, it is already happening, with companies like Virgin declaring its entry into the telecommunications market and the hitherto grey world of financial services. Such is the affection people in the UK feel for the brand, and for the clarity of Richard Branson's vision for Virgin as the 'people's champion' and 'cartel-buster', that it tends to be forgiven for the occasional overstretch. And indeed Virgin is positively welcomed into new categories.

At the other end of the technology spectrum, Apple holds deeper and more special relationships with some of its customers than any other brand. But if one looks at the different types of values that create strong all-round relationships, it is evident that until recently Apple had lost power in some of these areas. While Apple continued to enjoy an extraordinarily strong brand position both at the most profound level of *central* values, and at the *expressive* values level of user individuality, the brand suffered difficulties in its *functional* values. It is fascinating to see how the launch of the iMac has both 'repaired' the functional value problems that Apple has had and renewed the way in which people connect with its vision and values.

Of the other brands 'bubbling under' the top 25 in both brand value and brand strength, a few stand out for special comment. Gap is a relatively new global brand, with a full set of winning characteristics: clarity and distinctiveness of values, absolute consistency of application, and leadership in product development and total brand experience.

Both Moët & Chandon and Louis Vuitton appear lower down in the top 50 of the world's most valuable brands league table, but climb into the top 10 alongside Coca-Cola and Gillette when one looks at their brand value as a multiple of brand revenue. This table (Figure 3) lists companies that enjoy the highest leverage from their brands. So desirable and valuable have the Moët & Chandon and Louis Vuitton brands become in their customers' minds that both of them generate a brand value more than twice the revenue they create.

* Multiples of revenues are a recognised measurement for comparing the relative value of financial assets. Brand value as a multiple of brand revenue indicates the relative value creation of the brands. The multiple is calculated by dividing brand value by last year's reported brand revenue. A brand with a high multiple can extract relatively more value from its brand than a brand with a lower multiple. The above table shows the highest relative brand value creators.

This list excludes high tech companies which show very high multiples. However, these multiples represent growth rates of the underlying business.

Figure 3	The world's most valuable brands Brand value as a multiple of brand revenue*	
	Brand	**Multiple**
1	Coca-Cola	4.95
2	Gillette	3.83
3	Louis Vuitton	2.35
4	Nescafé	2.21
5	Wrigley's	2.20
6	Marlboro	2.16
7	McDonald's	2.11
8	Möet & Chandon	2.09
9	Barbie	1.98
10	Kleenex	1.98

Source: Interbrand/Citibank

Brand challenges

Whichever way you look at it, brands today are the most demonstrably powerful and sustainable wealth creators in the world. The term 'brand' and the practice of branding are not only being applied across the full spectrum of businesses; they are now being applied across any type of organisation that seeks to create a relationship with its audiences over and above day-to-day process and cost. This brand education and 'conversion' process is extensive, but perhaps not yet complete. In order to thrive, and in order to create greater wealth and influence not only for companies, but for countries, organisations and their people, brands need the support of governments and opinion formers – in both attitudes and policy. There still seems to be an element of suspicion in certain quarters of the media, arts and public services about the nature of branding, or perhaps about it being a rather cosmetic or superficial activity.

One role for brand experts over the next 25 years may be to continue the evangelism about the power and real value of brands to make beneficial contributions to people's lives – professionally, personally and to society in general.

It will also be up to brand owners and creators to look ahead to some of the likely changes in the business world in the next century, as well as wider trends in society, and to ensure that they are creating, managing or re-developing their brands to be at the forefront of those changes – wherever in the world they are.

There is no getting away from the fact that, in an increasingly blurred and virtual future, just about *everything and everyone is capable of becoming a brand*. Any brand future needs to address how to be a better, stronger, more distinctive and more valued brand in the round. In the final chapter, we discuss 10 observations and possibilities for brands in this future.

EMERGING TRENDS

Our contributors were asked for their wide-ranging views on brands today, on changes in society, and about possible brand stars of the future.

The discussion outline was tailored to specialisms, but broadly covered the following questions:
- What is your understanding of 'brand'?
- Which brands do you believe are the greatest in the world today?
- Do you have any personal favourite brands?
- What is your best and worst-case vision of society in 25 years' time?
- Which great brands today do you think will still be great in 25 years' time?
- Which ones may fail, and why?
- Are there any lesser-known or regional/local brands today that you feel may be among the world's greatest in 25 years' time?
- Which types of brands, or which categories, do you feel may yield great new brands in the future?

Considering the diversity of backgrounds, surprisingly strong common themes emerge: for instance the definition of brands in terms of *relationships*, *two-way communications*, *friendship*, *trust*. For many of our contributors, Coca-Cola is the most widely admired brand today – particularly in its capacity to refresh itself as well as its consumers, and its ability to touch a universal nerve. Disney is widely cited as the best example of a 'hero' brand across categories – and, for many, a future world's greatest brand.

Gap, Pampers, Nike, Virgin, Apple, Starbucks, Amazon.com, and Yahoo! all get multiple mentions – for being both strong brands now, and future 'greats'.

Perhaps the most interesting comments arise in discussion of Microsoft, McDonald's and CNN. Microsoft is widely admired for its phenomenal growth; however, while some have complete confidence in its future, others muse on the need to build the Microsoft *brand*, rather than the *business* of the brand. Otherwise, understandable concerns about the future commodification of technology emerged. McDonald's is, as always, admired for its consistency and universality; but its future is sometimes queried on those grounds, too. Will the brand refresh and renew itself vigorously enough to retain its position in the future? Or will it become too predictable and 'off trend' in a world as hungry for different experiences as for the familiar?

Again, CNN is widely admired for its original risk-taking vision, and for a future of extraordinary possibilities in the age of the information brand. Its challenge, for our contributors, is really to maintain its leadership position and to be people's most trusted and desired brand *editor* in the information age.

Other common themes emerging in people's hopes, dreams and concerns about the future involve the inevitable convergence and homogenisation of world cultures. And, of course, the parallel force to this: an increasing drive to retain local and personal identities.

The most widespread concerns for the future are over inequalities in society – both at the national and international level. Many contributors paint a nightmare scenario where a 'fast track' developed world begins to exist in a 'drawbridge society', separate from an increasingly alienated (and armed) developing world.

Against this, the hopes for society are about freedom and individual empowerment through information, education and knowledge. Also, about the importance of passion, humanity, benevolence and social responsibility shown by business, to all its stakeholders, above and beyond the profit motive.

For our contributors, the most fertile areas for great brand development appear in: *personal information management*; *health and well-being* (both in personal fitness and more holistic, 'alternative' forms); *leisure*, *hospitality* and *entertainment*, born from the need to 'retreat' and repair from stressed-out lives; the *'new' sciences of genetics and biotechnology*; and last but not least, *education* for a new generation of world citizens.

Overall, there is a strong sense of the potential for life-editing and life-simplifying brands; we might call them *hero* or *leader* brands, which provide a whole range of 'best of best' services for their busy audiences' lives. We will discuss the concept of such brands later, and which brands have the potential relationships to gain *share of mind* rather than just *share of shelf* in the future, as Mike Clasper of Procter & Gamble describes it.

We hope that you enjoy reading the individual contributors as much as we enjoyed our conversations with them.

Twenty-five visions

"Dream big and believe in your dreams."

Howard Schultz is Chairman and Chief Executive Officer of Starbucks Coffee Company. He joined Starbucks as Director of Operations & Marketing in 1982. Impressed by the popularity of espresso bars in Italy, he saw the potential to develop a similar coffee-bar culture in Seattle. In 1986 he left to start up his own chain of Italian style espresso bars and returned in 1987 to purchase Starbucks Coffee Company with the help of local investors. Today Starbucks is the world's leading retailer, roaster and brand of speciality coffee, with more than 2,100 retail locations in the US, the Far East and Europe.

"THE DEFINITION of a brand is probably more complex today than it ever has been. And what I specifically mean by that is that a brand has to feel like a friend. People have more choices today than they've ever had before and so I believe that a brand must be a bridge of trust to the consumer. Trust is definitely the future of brands.

WE LIVE IN a world today that is one giant commercial, and the customer by and large does not believe the message anyway. I would submit that there is probably, more than ever before, a lack of trust about public institutions and corporate America. And as a result of that, I think the rules of engagement have changed. There are three attributes that are more relevant than ever before in terms of these new standards of engagement for brands. And I mentioned the first one, trust. Second, we must build hope with our people, the people who do the work and the people who represent the company. More than ever before, people want to have a relationship with a company, and the company is represented by its people. So, if you build trust with the customer, hope with your people, the third attribute is community. And by that I mean that there has to be a sense of *benevolence*. A company today has to have a balance, and that balance is benevolence: giving back to the community and building community. If you maintain trust with your customer, hope with your people, and build community, you're not going to need the traditional forms of advertising. Because innately in the equity of the brand there's going to be this reservoir of goodwill. And that is how Starbucks has built its business.

OUR BRAND is deeply rooted in coffee obviously, but it means much, much more to us internally, and, I believe, to our customers. I think that Starbucks has become the 'third place' in all the communities in which we do business. And what I mean by that is the place between home and work. We have delivered something to the customer that's very important in their lives, and that is a great cup of coffee. We've also become a gathering place. And the romance of coffee and what we do has become an extension of people's front porch in the way they use our stores. We have built one of the most powerful brands in America, and soon the world, in a very unconventional manner: without traditional or significant advertising campaigns. So we are in a unique position because the level of trust that I spoke about before has been built on the experience that people have in our stores. And 9 million customers go through our stores every week, and the average customer comes back 18 times a month. We believe that the relationship that we built with our customers in our stores can be leveraged for other products in other channels of distribution. We have the number one coffee ice cream in America, we have the lead position in bottled Frappuccino, and now we're bringing Starbucks to the grocery aisle.

THERE HAS BEEN a tidal wave of change prompted by the World Wide Web; it's a new channel of

"A brand has to feel like a friend."

distribution breaking all the rules. And larger than life brands have emerged there in record time. So on one hand you have the great brands of the last 25 to 50 years that I think are still relevant and still delivering aspirational value, Coca-Cola, IBM and so on. Then on the other side you have companies that have broken all the rules, Yahoo!, America Online, eBay, Amazon, companies which have built an online community. And again I go back to trust. Through the Web they've been able to build an allegiance with their constituency in a much faster period than the traditional brands of the last 25 years, and, in doing so, have become more relevant. I don't believe that a company that ignores the Web can maintain its leadership position in its core category. We're committed to being a leader in the category, and the category will go beyond coffee. So we're going to recognise early the power of our brand to move our physical community over to the Web, and be one of the first bricks and mortar companies to fully integrate its Web strategy.

BUT REALLY, the question for brands is the sustainability of their trust factor, either online or via other channels. Let me give you my own personal theory, since I've been involved with two Internet companies, eBay and drugstore.com, in their embryonic stages. I think there's going to be a time, and I think sooner rather than later, when the physical and the online world come together. I think the best thinkers of the day are going to recognise that the consumer doesn't spend 24 hours online, the consumer does many different things. And for brands to really integrate themselves into the lifestyle of the consumer post-millennium, they're going to have to do it via many different channels, just to make sure they interact emotionally with the customer, wherever they are.

ONE OF THE great things about the future is that there are no rules. It's a very exciting time; you don't have to take the road that has been travelled before. Breaking the rules is part of the Starbucks culture; we like it, we enjoy it. We don't want to do what has been done before. Dream big and believe in your dreams. I grew up on the other side of the tracks, and for me to be in this place, surrounded by such talented people, should be a message to many young people that it can be done. But don't dream your dreams in a way that's confined to your own success. Success must be shared. So leave your ego at the door and surround yourself with people who are more talented, more experienced, more skilled than you are, so that collectively you can build a business in an enduring way. And, you know, success is not an entitlement, it has to be earned. There are many businesses that have gotten as far as we have, and then gone under because they lose touch with their core business and their customer.

I ALSO BELIEVE that the advantage we have over traditional brands is based on the fact that our customers see themselves inside our company, inside our brand, because they're part of the Starbucks *experience*, as opposed to a traditional branded product that is bought over the counter.

IBM
From the 1950s, IBM led the way in computer technology and the brand was in fact synonymous with the computer, promising technological leadership, reliability and quality. However, new entrants into the marketplace threatened the company's position, with consumers arguing that the brand had become arrogant and expensive. The appointment of Louis V Gerstner as CEO in 1993 saw IBM return to its core values and maximise its ability to provide customers with integrated business solutions combining products, technologies and services. IBM now strives to 'Make IT easy'.

"One of the great things about the future is that there are no rules."

And we want to leverage that experience in many different ways in the future. For instance, I think people are going to respond more and more to the things that are skewed towards the home. The family, personal relationships and achieving balance in one's life are going to be more important than ever, because there's been so much pressure and so much pull on our personal time from our work life. And everyone I talk to, my friends, my peers, I think we all recognise that there has to be balance in one's life to achieve the things we want. I think the whole area of health and wellness is going to be extremely relevant in the future. And I go back to the home. Products and services that focus on adding value to your family, to entertainment at your home, will be important, because I think that's where America is going to be spending more time. So to be relevant in 25 years' time, we want to live inside people's houses, to be a trusted friend inside their homes. And we're in a fortunate position that most people start their day drinking a cup of coffee; either at home or hopefully in a Starbucks store. Or take ice cream as another example. We've created flavours that bring a smile to people's faces when they eat, and enjoyment to their life. It's a little thing, but that carton of ice cream on the table with the family means that we are part of people's lives. And we want to continue to do those kinds of things. We don't want to be a one-dimensional component of their life, we want to share moments with them.

I THINK the world needs leaders. I'm a voracious reader of history, and if you look at the leaders in our parents' generation, they were larger than life. But now, there's no Winston Churchill, there's no FDR. Kids need heroes. There are events that have destroyed trust: the lock out in the NBA, what went on with the president, what's happened in Kosovo, all these things I think invalidate a promise. And I think it's critically important that people emerge who are both leaders and heroes who can meet our expectations, instead of constantly disappointing us. I found it fascinating myself that America and the world celebrated and mourned with such zeal the loss of Joe DiMaggio. But what they were so hungry for was not his baseball feats 50 years ago, but what he stood for. Nowadays, we don't see grace, we don't see humility, we don't see leadership, we don't see responsibility. And in the future, that will be as much a part of building a brand as anything else."

Starbucks
Starbucks Coffee Company was founded In 1971 in Seattle, originally selling only coffee beans. It was not until Howard Schultz, today's Chairman, joined Starbucks in the early 1980s that the idea of the American coffee bar really took off. Schultz was inspired by his experience of espresso bars in Italy to create what he called a 'third place' – not home or work – in which people could relax. Today Starbucks has around 2,100 retail locations in North America, Asia and the UK. The company is renowned not only for its innovations in coffee retailing, but also for its enlightened employment practices and its charitable Starbucks Foundation.

"When everything's working well, it's not easy to leave your position of security and step into the future."

Karl-Heinz Kalbfell is Global Head of Brand and Product Strategy for BMW Group. Following a Masters in Marketing & Engineering, he undertook further studies in Business Management & Economics at Stuttgart University. In 1977 he joined the Marketing Communications team at BMW. His responsibilities have included positions as Head of International Exhibitions, Head of International Marketing Programmes, International Brand and Product Communication and National Advertising, President of BMW M GmbH and Director of Marketing for BMW Group. He was promoted to his current position in 1999.

"FOR ME, a brand is a clear value signal, a promise of style and quality. Really, at its core, branding is simply marking something and saying, 'This is from me'. You can see it when you watch the kids on the streets with their skateboards and fancy T-shirts; they're wearing a lifestyle. It's not easy to choose the greatest brand in the world, but I think one of the greatest is Marlboro. It's been strong for decades and has such a consistent presence worldwide. It's amazing. I admire its authenticity, its worldwide communication. It's one of the really big global players. I find it hard to name a personal favourite brand. I work in the automotive business, and in many ways I'd like to pick my own brand, BMW, but that's not fair. It's such a big part of my life!

I'M VERY LUCKY to be working with one of the world's greatest brands. It's thrilling. It's also hard work of course. Going back to what I said about Marlboro, it's not easy to maintain that kind of worldwide consistency. We live in a world where lots of new ideas appear all the time, but in order to keep a brand strong and consistent, sometimes you have to ignore new ideas. To keep the brand's core values going can occasionally seem dull; that's why you have to be tough to succeed. And the greater the number of people working in a company, the harder it becomes to keep the brand consistent. Central to BMW's success is the excitement we all feel about what we do. When everyone in the company shares that excitement, you don't really need to convince them of the importance of the brand. That's why I invest a lot of time in keeping people informed about things like the launch of new advertising campaigns.

IN SOME WAYS, though, when you've got a strong, consistent brand image, it can make it difficult to move forward. When everything's working well, it's not easy to leave your position of security and step into the future. We're constantly struggling with that balance – innovation on the one hand, consistency on the other. The main challenge for us in the future is to be ahead of the changes in society. We need a combination of internal and external thinking to drive the brand forward – engineers, marketeers and long-term, probing market research. The car is going to become increasingly important in society over the next 25 years. Individual mobility will grow rapidly because it's central to the freedom of the human being. And tied into this is people's need to be different. When you look at all the mergers in the automotive industry, it seems that their main target is to be big. I think they're forgetting one thing – because people want to be different, they don't want mass products. So when something becomes mass, it becomes a problem.

I THINK the core values of BMW will still be strong 25 years from now, but the solutions that the brand offers might be a little bit different. The demand for clean energy will certainly affect brand development. Today's consumers are also demanding security, easy living, easy moving. We claim today that our cars are like tight fitting Italian suits. Everything has to fit perfectly. That's one of the

"Condensed information for the individual is what the future's about."

greatest challenges for automotive engineering. Car manufacturing is a very high volume business, but people now demand complete individualisation. Consumers will also be looking for fun and entertainment, not just the rational side of life. BMW's emotional values give it an advantage here.

THIRTY YEARS AGO the basic values of BMW were sportiness and innovation with a niche status. BMW entered this very small niche in order to differentiate its products. That's been one of the secrets of BMW's success. But the idea of finding a niche for a brand has now entered the mainstream of marketing, finding ways to suit the lifestyle of relevant target groups has now become the major challenge. It's up to us to decide how to keep BMW's values relevant for the years to come. I think it's very important to keep track of semantics, so we do a lot of work in that area. If you asked people 20 years ago what they understood by sportiness, they would have said something completely different from people today. At BMW we take the same words and ask what people see behind them. One of the core words we use is *dynamism*. What will *dynamism* mean in 25 years? That's something we have to consider very deeply.

I THINK brands act as a kind of guideline for humans. In fact, people want to be guided. Look at the software industry or at sports products – product life cycles are becoming shorter and shorter, so brand messages need to be very clear. The proliferation of information sources – the Internet, special interest magazines – means that people are grateful for those clear messages, even if they don't express it that way themselves. They don't need to think about why they choose Coca-Cola or Nike, they see other people they admire choosing those brands and that makes it easier for them. People are attracted by lifestyle expressions; when kids see Michael Jordan advertising Nike, they think 'This product suits me and I want to be related to it.' And if kids act like this, it works thoughout the family.

COMMUNICATIONS ARE central to the development of brands. There is so much information around, and the challenge now is how to make it useful and accessible. You need to be able to push a button and get all the information you need. The problem with newspapers is that 90 per cent of them aren't of interest to you. Condensed information for the individual is what the future's about.

I WOULD PICK Coca-Cola as a brand that will still be great in 25 years' time. They really understand the whole business of creating a lifestyle. After all, there's very little that's innovative about the actual product now, and you can't do anything with it but drink it. But it's become a lifestyle, not just a drink. Of course BMW will still be great; it understands lifestyle too. It's not fair to talk about competitors, though I'd definitely pick Mercedes.

I DON'T WANT TO name individual brands that I think won't make it in the future, but I can identify

BMW
BMW is based in Munich and has a worldwide reputation for advanced technology, excellent product quality and fine styling. The company began life in 1916 as an aircraft manufacturer and, indeed, the blue and white BMW badge originates from a stylised propeller. BMW is renowned for its strong corporate branding, which is manifested by the consistency of all BMW international offices and showrooms. BMW's ambition over the last eight decades has been to design and manufacture vehicles that are always the 'ultimate driving machine'. The company is proud of its tradition and is committed to a set of powerful and timeless values.

"We will want brands which offer fun, comfort, satisfaction; we won't just want to work."

what type of brands they will be – brands which aren't strong enough to be consistent, brands with insecure management. When brands are discounted because business is not going well, it's the beginning of the end. If you reduce prices, you will ruin the brand; either you won't make a profit, or the brand will fail because it will be seen to have cheated people, to have had no real substance. I think some of the fashion brands are in real danger, and I think that a lot of software companies will disappear too. I need to be careful in my position when naming brands – everyone is a potential customer of BMW! So I have to wish success to everyone.

THE ENTERTAINMENT INDUSTRY is one to watch for the next 25 years. Now that all the countries of the world and all the things in the universe have been discovered, people definitely want to be entertained. If I didn't work for BMW, I would certainly pursue a career in entertaining people. Similarly, I think health and fitness brands will be very important. How can a 70 year old woman look young? How can you live a full and dynamic life at 70? We will want brands which offer fun, comfort, satisfaction; we won't just want to work like hell. In the future, if people are less stressed, there'll be less pressure; I think this will have a political dimension – there'll be less risk of political crisis.

WHATEVER HAPPENS, the next 25 years are going to be thrilling and, in the automotive industry, very challenging. We already face extremely strong competition and only the strongest will survive. On a wider scale, I know that I would like to see one worldwide standard of living. Of course, that's a human dream. But – and it's hard to say this – it would also be great for BMW's international business!

A GREAT BRAND of the future? Well, 20 years ago it was unheard of for people to eat organic food, to go to an organic farm to buy their food. That's a very interesting development. Perhaps in 25 years we'll be able to buy special air from Nepal. There are strong drinking water brands today, like Evian, so in the future we might have branded air – you never know! That idea reminds me of something I read recently, something about a successful businesswoman whose passion is self-collected rainwater for her garden. It's tempting to see things like that as signals of what the future holds."

Evian

Evian Natural Mineral Water is bottled direct at its source in Evian-les-Bains, on the shores of Lake Geneva in the French Alps. The spring was first discovered during the French Revolution by the Marquis de Lessert, who believed that the water helped to cure his ailments, and in the following years the town became a popular spa resort. Evian was first bottled in 1826; today, 4 million litres of Evian water are bottled each day and exported to more than 120 countries around the world. The brand is packaged in a unique sculpted bottle, reminiscent of Alpine scenery, which is designed to encourage recycling.

"In the next 25 years, the debate will be about making capitalism more humane."

Will Hutton, Editor in Chief of *The Observer*, has been at the forefront of British political and economics journalism for 20 years. As a producer and correspondent at the BBC in the 80s he worked on Newsnight, The Money Programme and Financial World Tonight. In 1990 he joined *The Guardian* as Economics Editor and was appointed Assistant Editor in 1995; the following year he became Editor of *The Observer*. Awarded 'Political Journalist of the Year' by Granada TV in 1993, his book *The State We're In* was published in 1995 and has remained in the best-seller lists ever since.

"I SEE BRANDS as intrinsic to a rather different understanding of how a market economy works. My understanding of a brand is at two levels. At one level plainly, it's about distinguishing your products from competitors, but what lies behind that is a much deeper statement about the nature of market capitalism and about what makes a successful company. It overlaps with my notion of stakeholder society. I don't believe that a company is just a series of ad hoc contracts between the people who manage it and the people who work for it, or between shareholders and the 'company'. A company is much, much more than that. It's a social organisation which embodies a value system. And the reason why great brands are durable is because the companies that produce them are themselves social organisations that exist over time. The brand captures the notion that there's an on-going relationship between the buyer, the customer and the producer, and there are values behind the brand that you're buying into when you buy the product. People dislike the sense that market capitalism is commoditising everything, your holiday, your marriage, your death. And actually what a brand says is, 'Hey, this isn't a commodity. There's an idea in here which is actually independent of the price you're paying.'

I PASSIONATELY BELIEVE in stakeholder capitalism. If you just think capitalism is about the money nexus, you don't get it. You have to force boardrooms to think in terms of the people they have working for them and the need to sustain their loyalty. It's all a bit more complicated than 'pile them high, sell them cheap, hire, fire, I take tough decisions', all those stereotypes associated with being a successful capitalist. You have to say, 'Hold on a minute, is that actually the essence of what's going on in this company? Why does this company exist? Why was it here 25 years ago? Why will it be here in 25 years' time?' So I think that behind good brands lie stakeholder companies, or at least companies which actually put some time and effort into investing in their relationships.

FOR THAT REASON, I'd be very happy to apply my idea of brand to political parties. A political party is about entering a relationship. It's about trust. It's about delivery. The right approach is to say 'I have values which require me to build a political narrative, to do the things I believe in. And that political narrative needs to be expressed in words which people in focus groups tell me would be more easily understood.' What I dislike intensely is turning political processes inside out through thinking in 'brand' terms. The wrong way to think about a political brand is to allow it to be defined by what you imagine people want you to say; in that way you become de-anchored as a political party. From a personal point of view, there are brands I like and with which I have a relationship of trust. I like Armani as a brand – I have Armani spectacles and an Armani suit. I like Renault as a car brand. If I had to single out my favourite brand, I think it would be Kellogg's, because Kellogg's cereals have never let me down. Since the age of 2 or 3, they've been absolutely consistent, you get what you want. I associate Kellogg's with this sunshine breakfast, it's there subliminally in my head, I can't

"Behind good brands lie stakeholder companies."

escape it. So I would always buy Kellogg's over own label brands; I resent it when other brands are bought, and I enjoy my breakfast cereal that much more because it's Kellogg's. The other brand I should mention is Gillette. I've tried Wilkinson, I've tried others and I always come back to Gillette. I'm absolutely sold on Gillette razors and I refuse to buy own brand shaving gel. What is that about? Again, I started my relationship with Gillette when I was 15 or 16 and they have a commitment to high quality; there's also the association of being freshly shaven, which I really like.

GREAT BRANDS capture an idea of reputation and this is increasingly important because I think we are seeing the general collapse of tradition and deference. I think we're seeing that status must be earned, not ascribed. Over the last 25 years the debate has been about socialism, communism and free market capitalism; in the next 25 years the debate will be about making capitalism more humane. At the moment, everyone feels disempowered because there's no supra-national government to control the global corporations who run our lives, and that we are simply disempowered victims of markets.

I THINK THE worst part of society in 25 years' time could be a massive growth in inequality. An elite living in a drawbridge society, opted out of everything, and living as individuals without constructing durable networks of friends. At the bottom, there could be a huge underclass which has also opted out and in the middle, a lower-middle class trying to keep things going in suburbia. All those strands are there at the moment. That kind of society would make it impossible to hold together public goods like public health and education and transport, which require us all to pay into a common pool because we all share those goods.

MY BEST VISION is that we literally reinvent ourselves with a tremendous sense of self-empowerment, and that everybody has access to information. Everyone has a series of different careers during the course of their life, and there's an aggregation of friendships from one career to another. Similarly with relationships: men and women become truly equal. We use information technology to open up decision-making, open up democracy, open up engagement. And in doing this, we understand that there really are public goods and things we hold in common that we must sustain.

I BELIEVE THAT brands and branding do have a part to play in the creation of this society. One of the things about poverty and inequality is that they're drab; they don't move on, they're always the same. We want to devise ways of helping people earn their way to a better life, rather than just handing them benefits. But the poor are always with us, and obviously these social problems are not as glamorous as the opening night of a film première with Elizabeth Hurley in a beautiful dress. The

Kellogg's

Back in the twenties, the general public consumed vast quantities of egg, bacon and porridge every morning. In those days, the very idea of shaking ready cooked food from a packet, and just adding milk, was totally unknown. In 1924, however, Kellogg's set up a company in the British Isles and Kellogg's Corn Flakes were introduced to a suspicious public. From then on, breakfast cereals became part of everyday life and Kellogg's is now synonymous with health and vitality. Early packets carried the words 'Only The Original Has This Signature', and to this day the famous Kellogg's logo is based on the signature of WK Kellogg, the company's founder.

"I think we are seeing the general collapse of tradition and deference."

story doesn't change. Wars move on. Politics moves on. Corporations move on. A football match or great cricket match, there's a winner or loser. Poverty and inequality are just there. And actually what brands can do is relieve that boredom. The charisma of a brand can break through all that. Or branding could be used just to liven up state initiatives!

I THINK WHAT'S made successful brands in the past will be even more true of brands in the future. For example, The Financial Times is successful as a brand, not just because it's bound up with high quality information but because being a reader of The Financial Times is a statement about oneself. Now that's always been the case with brands, but I think that will become more so. Brands have got to be about individualisation and about individual empowerment; brands must enrich your life choices, and I think it's one reason why designer clothes have done so well. Winners and losers of the future? Marlboro I worry about from a personal point of view! I think McDonald's may be losing it, actually. I took my children to McDonald's the other day and thought, 'I'm not sure about this set up'. Hamburgers are kind of tiresome now; McDonald's are locked into hamburgers and hamburgers are a mature market. They only grow by actually opening up lots of new sites, but they're reaching saturation point. Also, the hamburger is too commoditised a product. They can't empower customers any more. In the beginning, McDonald's started to empower customers, by giving them something very nice, really quick, which they hadn't had before. The brand added to the variety of life; it was good fun to take the kids there. But we've done that now, we've had the experience, we want to move on.

IN THE FUTURE, I think any brand to do with personal fitness or prolongation of the idea of beauty will be a real winner, because we're going to have high disposable incomes and the time to worry about those issues. Something like La Prairie I think will be a winning brand on a 10 or 20 year view, if it's managed correctly. Also Venturi fitness machines. I think it has lots of scope. Boots is a brand that's underdeveloped in terms of what it might be able to deliver. Educational brands, like Penguin and Dorling Kindersley – those are great. Education, health, personal fitness, personal appearance, I think are going to be the areas we'll see great brands of the future emerge from. But they've got to respect the moral obligation that underpins all successful human exchange. Successful brands will be the ones that actually get that story right."

Penguin

The first ten Penguin paperback titles were printed in 1935 and included works by Agatha Christie, Ernest Hemingway and Compton Mackenzie. Penguin was the brainchild of Allen Lane, who had realised that there was a gap in the market for affordable quality literature. Lane wanted a 'dignified but flippant' name for his company, and it was his secretary who suggested the penguin. Over the years Penguin has been no stranger to controversy, having published among other works *Lady Chatterley's Lover*, *Spycatcher* and *The Satanic Verses*; today it remains one of the world's leading paperback publishers.

"I would label the consumer of 2025 in three ways: more demanding, wiser and more worried."

Mike Clasper is President of Global Home Care and New Business Development at Procter & Gamble Europe. Educated at St John's College, Cambridge, he joined Procter & Gamble's marketing department in 1978 and has held key management posts in the UK and Western Europe prior to his most recent appointment. Active in the environmental community, Mike is a member of the Advisory Committee on Business and the Environment and chairs the Sustainable Production and Consumption sub-group; he also sits on the Advisory Board for the Institute of Management Studies at Cambridge University.

"TO START WITH, THE FUTURE of brands is definitely global. You can't market a brand in one way in North America and another in the UK and expect it to be a secret; consumers talk to each other on channels like Internet chatlines. And that includes the developing world. I think the developing world will go online much more quickly than we think. I was in a 20sq metre home in Mexico City with 5 people in it, and they had a colour television. That colour television can turn into a desktop, into an Internet connection, for a percentage of the cost of the television. Why wouldn't they be on the net in 10 or 15 years' time, even if they're still in the 20sq metre home?

THIS WILL DRIVE one of the 2 mega-trends that are going to heavily influence the consumer of the future. The first one is the absolute explosion of access to knowledge, which is triggered by the Internet. The second mega-trend is the robustness of the world economy. If you take a macro-economic view, we've never seen the sort of golden age of growth that we've had over the last 10 years. I think that's been driven by the change in the world political structure in which free trade is assumed to be the way forward. This will continue to create wealth at a consistent pace that we haven't seen in the past.

AS A RESULT of these trends, I would label the consumer of 2025 in three ways: more demanding, wiser and more worried. And brands are going to have to respond to this. Let me talk about the demanding area first. I think that has two broad elements: (1) higher demands and (2) broader demands. Higher demands first. The brand's going to have to perform its basic function much better than it's done in the past. It's going to have to move from purely satisfying to delighting consumers. And consumers' demands are also going to be broader. Consumers are time-starved; they're going to demand easier ways of doing things, and it's going to have to be more aesthetically pleasing as well. I think that what the iMac has done is purely wonderful, a brilliant example of what I'm talking about, and I would love to be able to do that with all my brands. I'd love to give them aesthetic designer appeal as part of the total package without detracting one jot from how good they are at a basic functional level.

PEOPLE WILL ALSO want easy access via every possible distribution channel, including e-commerce. To meet this type of demand, we need to think about extending physical brands into services. Xerox says, 'We provide copies, not copy machines'. If I have a fear for FMCG companies, it's the fact that they're currently built around the physical and if they don't find ways of stepping beyond that, then they're liable to become suppliers of somebody else's brands, ingredients of a service brand. And I don't want to only supply HomeCleaning.com! One consequence of this breadth of offering from a brand will be a world of many more alliances, because it won't be possible or desirable to provide all the elements yourself.

"We've never seen the sort of golden age of growth that we've had over the last ten years."

SO THAT'S what I mean by 'more demanding'. Now let's move onto the 'wiser' and 'worried', which are both going to come from the knowledge explosion. Consumers are going to be able to benchmark the things that they want to buy, because lots of companies on the Internet will run businesses comparing things. In a sense it's Which? magazine multiplied a thousand times and readily accessible at home. People are also going to want, and be able, to find out a lot about the citizenship of a brand, whether it's doing the right things socially, economically, environmentally. That information will be provided either by the company itself or by NGOs. That's what I mean by 'wiser'.

NOW 'MORE WORRIED'. Well, there's a clear trend towards much greater concern about health. There are direct health concerns – 'Is this thing good for me?' But there are also a lot of indirect health concerns. There's this sense of, 'We're letting the genie out of the bottle. There's an irreversible process going on and we can't stop it.' Climate change has that sense of irreversibility. These concerns will be fuelled by chat rooms on the Internet. The ability of small pressure groups to create an explosion of activity around a particular subject is frightening. It's also very easy to create a false Internet rumour; a single chat room has started a rumour about one of our brands that spread to around 5 per cent of the population. One single chat room and a huge discussion of a totally false issue! So I think the consumer is going to be faced with lots of rumours and lots of concerns.

WHAT ARE brands going to do about all this? Well, as I've said, brands of 2025 will have to offer more, and offer it better. Brands will need to win the battle for share of mind, not share of shelf. And I think there are only 2 ways in which an individual brand will win. They'll either be personally customised or they'll be a confident, no worry choice. Customisation is a challenge, because, although it's easy to see how you can afford to tailor a $1,000 computer, I'm not sure it's sensible for a brand to have 2,000 types of individually designed shampoos. If you go the confident choice route, value superiority and easy access are vital. Brands like this will succeed because the consumer will value not having to think about alternatives.

COMPANIES ARE going to need to ensure that these wiser yet concerned consumers can 'investigate' the brand. If I dream to 2025, there' s no reason why a sensor chip on the packaging couldn't provide all the data that a consumer might be interested in. On top of this, brands are going to come with information that will enhance them. For physical brands, it might be information to enable the consumer to customise how they used the product. For appliances, it might be information that made the use of the product far easier and more delightful. I don't think it will be long before you'll have a chip on an appliance which talks you through the basics, instead of a 50 page book in 10 languages.

Xerox
Founded in 1906, Xerox has become a household name, although its operations have moved far beyond its photocopier roots. Today, Xerox is The Document Company – the world's leading provider of global document solutions. It offers unrivalled expertise in the production and management of all types of document: colour and black and white, paper and digital, for home offices or global enterprises. These solutions help customers to compete through the effective management and sharing of knowledge. Employing 91,400 people worldwide, Xerox generated revenues of $19.4bn in 1998 and invests around 6% of its worldwide revenues in research and development.

"Brands will need to win the battle for share of mind, not share of shelf."

WHAT ABOUT my bets for the big brands of 2025? There are going to be a lot more information brands. Yahoo! today is already a brand that's meeting the needs of the 'wise' and 'worried', the need for easy access to knowledge. Amazon.com is a brand meeting the needs of the time-starved. I can choose books and records when I want; I don't need to go to a store or read a review or anything. A brand like Amazon.com is a real leader – they can analyse my choices, and then predict which five books I'll probably like, which all reinforces my relationship with them. As far as the confident choice brands are concerned, brands like Fairy Liquid and Ariel will need to get into that position. Fairy Liquid is a brand I have great nostalgia for – it's everything that a dishwashing product should be.

I WOULD SAY Disney is a great brand which will survive and thrive in the next 25 years, because it already goes beyond its original function. Yes, it has the original element a Disney film has to work, it has to entertain. But it's also a retail channel and a theme park. Virgin is another brand which stands out because of its roundness. I think that top UK retailer brands have a good chance of making it, because they're already into customisation. They've started taking steps with their loyalty cards and their Internet shopping experiments. They know I like making pasta with tomato sauce, and they can tell me when they've got a good offer on tomatoes.

ALL THESE BIG brands of 2025 will need to address the wise, worried and more demanding consumer. They are going to move beyond the physical product, to be the person and the company behind the brand. I think consumers will expect companies to get fair rewards for their efforts but not to make obscene profits, to behave appropriately in a social sense. Things like employment charters around the world, what brands put back into the community. And doing the right thing by the planet, which means sustainable consumption and production. The Microsoft case in the US is about fair reward. Nike production in the Far East is a case of labour practices around the world under scrutiny. And the Shell Brent Spar incident is a classic case of 'must be seen to do right by the planet'. Companies will need to be more transparent so that consumers can reassure themselves about the sustainability of their brand choice. So over the next 25 years brand owners will also have to start thinking a little bit more deeply about their responsibilities."

Fairy Liquid

Procter & Gamble's Fairy Liquid first reached more progressive household sinks at the beginning of the 1960s. Today it is available on a worldwide basis. From the outset, mildness has been consistently maintained as the heart of the brand, and many people still remember the advertising: 'Now hands that do dishes can be as soft as your face'. The brand has always retained contemporary relevance, and in recent years has extended into related product areas, including dishwasher and detergent products. Most recently, Fairy Liquid Anti-bacterial has been introduced.

"The crucial thing
now is that people
want to feel good
about their way
of consuming."

Marieke van der Werf is a co-founder of communications agency New Moon, and mother of three young children. Marieke studied Dutch literature and language and is also a trained ballet teacher. For the last nine years she has specialised in communications focusing on environmental and internal issues, working as a senior consultant and partner for one of the Netherlands' largest PR agencies. In 1998 she started New Moon with like-minded colleagues who wanted to form a flexible consultancy specialising in the fields of social responsibility, IT and the environment.

"A BRAND IS A NAME that stands for something, that tells me something. What it tells me is very specific; it differentiates it from other brands. I know it's a cliché, but I would have to pick Coca-Cola as one of the world's greatest brands. It really is a classic and so much has been built into it. Another of my favourite brands is Ikea; it's an interesting brand to me both as a professional and as a consumer. I admire the way they have grown and developed the business. The products are good quality, simple and not too expensive, and they have thought about my needs. There's a bit of me that says 'Am I so obvious?' Well, perhaps I am! Ikea fulfils my needs and gives me ideas that are very helpful. Altogether it's a very transparent relationship.

I SUPPOSE I'm from the Ikea generation – my room as a teenager was fitted out with Ikea stuff. But what's great is the way that Ikea has moved along with me. Now that I have children myself, I appreciate the fact that there's a place for them to go, that I don't need to worry about them. Ikea is far more than just the products – it's the total experience. The concept of the shops is perfectly fitted to its customers. You couldn't accuse Ikea of being stupid or not thinking about something. Even though I might not always be completely pleased with the quality of the products, I accept it because I know it and you can always get stuff changed – it's part of the deal that you enter into with Ikea.

ANOTHER RETAIL brand that I really like is Albert Heijn – a chain of supermarkets here in the Netherlands. It's not the cheapest supermarket around, but they really understand their customers – people like me who grew up with the values of the 60s and 70s, but have also lived through the 80s and 90s. Albert Heijn offers quality goods in a luxurious atmosphere. There's a certain status attached to shopping there – you feel you've achieved something if you can do all your shopping at Albert Heijn. At the same time they seem to care for the environment and look after their employees; they always seem to employ people who fit in with the neighbourhood. The crucial thing now is that people want to feel good about their way of consuming. I think that Albert Heijn has achieved a good balance; they respect the social values built up in the 60s, but they allow us to indulge in the more materialistic things that we've come to enjoy in the last 2 decades.

I THINK THAT in general there is now an opportunity for brands to help their consumers not to feel guilty about their purchases. I mean, I'm not exactly an 'environmental activist', so I feel more comfortable shopping at Albert Heijn than at a health food store. But I trust Albert Heijn to make my choices for me. I think that the really strong brands are the ones that have done all the thinking for me. They've already made all the comparisons between different products, between means of production. I don't have to make the comparisons myself because they give me that assurance.

"Really strong brands are the ones which have done all my thinking for me."

CONSUMERS TODAY are increasingly looking for brands which will help them make responsible choices. We have such a good life in this part of the world and we don't want to give it up. People won't stop buying cars or televisions, because we can't really do without them now, but we're looking to brands to help take away some of the anxiety, to allow us to maintain our standard of living responsibly. A few new brands, like Ben & Jerry's, have understood this trend, but the majority of brands are reacting rather slowly or are just doing something because they feel they should.

THERE WAS a time when a company could be popular just because it was making money. There are some major Dutch brands, such as Shell and Philips, which have come from this tradition. I don't feel very warmly towards them at the moment, but I still believe that they will survive over the next 25 years because of the money, power and knowledge base within them. On the other hand companies can no longer just rely on those 'critical mass' things, they also have to have public sympathy. In order to survive they will have to shift their focus, but that's very hard for companies that have worked in set ways for so many years.

TAKE SHELL. They should be in an ideal position to develop products for the future – they have the money, the means, the knowledge. They could develop new ways of getting around, new ways of using energy. They could be working out how to take the burden of guilt away from the consumer. But it's terribly difficult for a company like that to adapt; it's like an oyster shell trying to open up. And with incidents like Brent Spar, people start to wonder whether they want to be associated with Shell any more. Yet we owe today's good standard of living, the achievements of the 90s, to companies like Shell. If these companies were to pay more attention to their social responsibility, they would have my loyalty. But they have to understand what kind of responsibility is involved, and they have to act quickly before they lose me, and others like me, forever.

ALL THIS MEANS that brands are becoming increasingly important in the world. A hundred years ago, even 40 years ago, people's priorities were different. Now people constantly discuss their work and work has become extremely important in determining people's identity. In the past, people built up their sense of personal identity from their family values, the church, clubs, but many of those influences have disappeared. To a large extent now people build up their identity from the companies they work for and from the brands they use.

JUST IMAGINE what it would do to people's sense of personal identity if they were excluded from using certain brands! It would be fascinating to investigate how someone would feel if they went to buy a television and then discovered that they had been banned from using the brand – effectively put on the black list for Sony or Philips. You could imagine that if you found out you were on the

Shell

The Royal Dutch/Shell Group was formed in 1907 and is today one of the world's largest businesses. Shell has recently suffered accusations of bad corporate citizenship for the handling of situations such as Brent Spar and its brand has suffered as a result. Possibly in response to these accusations, in October 1997 Shell established a 5th core business area, Renewables, which is intended to mark Shell's commitment to sustainable development. It is estimated that over the next 25 years between 5–10% of the world's energy will come from renewable resources, and over the next 5 years, Shell are investing $0.5bn in exploring these technologies.

"Just imagine what it would do to people's sense of personal identity if they were excluded from using certain brands!"

black list for Nike, you would start to doubt your own identity – what did you do wrong?

DIALOGUE WITH consumers is critical to all great and future brands. It's so simple – all these campaigns, all these managers thinking about how to get people to buy more and more products and to remain loyal, when all you need to do is ask them! In all these boardrooms everyone is trying to figure out what this target group or that set of consumers will want and the secret is just to stay in touch with them. It isn't enough just to talk to people, however; you have to know what to do with the answers. You have to be committed to solving the problems.

I SUPPOSE what I'm saying is that brand communication has to be a two-way process. In the long term the only viable brands will be listening brands. And listening brands are by their very nature less arrogant, more vulnerable, than brands which don't ask questions. A lot of today's top brands are rather arrogant. If they want to last they will have to become more vulnerable. A brand that I think will be big in the future? I would choose a new chain of hotels in Germany: Berghaus, Seehaus, Waldhaus. Their philosophy is to make your stay as comfortable and as real as possible. Instead of individually wrapped food and loads of packaging, there is real fresh food on the breakfast table, large fruit bowls and so on. They make your stay natural, authentic and personal.

I SET UP my own business because I wanted to work in a much closer and more personal way with my clients. But I was also looking for a new way of working – free from guilt. I have chosen a way of working that allows me to make room for my children, to consider their needs, to bring them into the office when that's appropriate. I think it will be vital for all businesses in the future to give people the space and flexibility to explore their passions both at home and at work – whether their passion is their family, their house, their sport. If people can't express their passions, they are not complete people."

Ikea

Ikea has a very simple, yet compelling vision: A better everyday life. Since its creation in 1943, the world-leading store has brought its practical, attractive and competitively priced furniture and accessories into millions of homes worldwide. The company's Swedish founder, Ingvar Kamprad, was only 17 when he set up his first mail-order business; he created the unusual name by combining his initials with the initials of the farm and the village where he grew up. The Ikea retail stores, with their striking blue and yellow logo, exemplify the company's focus on form and function; ample parking, good restaurants and excellent children's facilities.

"At the moment we're all so locked into the fact that we're supposed to have a phone, a credit card, a Porsche, a mortgage; we seem to have lost touch with things that come from the heart."

Paul Smith, whose business has an annual turnover of £173m, is Europe's most successful designer in Japan and remains in poll position in Britain. His introduction to the fashion industry was accidental, when, aged 18, without qualifications, his father secured him a job in a local clothing warehouse. In 1970 he opened his own shop in Nottingham and in 1976 he decided to go it alone, showing his first collection in Paris under the Paul Smith label. Today Paul Smith has shops in London, Nottingham, Manchester, New York, Paris, Hong Kong, Singapore, Taiwan, Manila and over 200 shops in Japan.

"I THINK IN many ways the world is now over-full of brands, over-full of hype, and over-full of information. The word 'brand' sometimes fills me with horror. And the fact that I'm possibly one myself is even more horrific! This is scary stuff! I'm realistic about the strength of brands; I just feel uncomfortable with their definition.

I'VE GOT a relatively big business in British fashion terms, although it's a small business in global terms, but it's always been very much about just designing clothes and talking to people. I don't think it has been a conscious thing at all, in any way, *ever*. It's always come from the heart; we've simply done what we've done, and luckily we've done okay. To me, brands often equate with very, very conscious effort, the effort of actually becoming a brand, of becoming something that is all about business and just making money. I'm not the VIP within the company; the customer is the person who spends hard-earned money on our product, and that's really important to remember. So self-conscious branding is quite alien to me.

I DON'T REALLY have any favourite brands and if I were to pick some from the air, then the ones that would spring to mind would be Coca-Cola, probably because it's been around for so long. Or Nike, because, until recently, it's been a sort of fashion/utility crossover brand, with support that's been modern and down to earth and appealing. The only brands that leap to mind in the fashion arena are Ralph Lauren or Armani, although those are not my personal favourites. Ralph Lauren has been brilliantly done, and I think basically the product is good. It's lacking a sense of humour but I'm a Brit and Brits tend to have a sense of humour! It sends out such a clear American marketing image, you know, buy a Polo shirt with a polo player on it and get a free stately home! And with Armani, you're buying into a sense of Italy and a particular Italian sensitivity. He's a very nice man who's achieved fantastic continuity, but unfortunately, he's recently lost his way a bit.

IN GENERAL, I tend not to be impressed by brands. It doesn't really penetrate my world at all, the brand. I almost *never* watch television and I rarely read newspapers. I wear all my own clothes because they're free, and I don't go out and think 'I'll buy that particular washing powder' – I don't buy washing powder! My car is a 1956 Bristol, because I like the shape of it. So really, I'm Mr Anti Brand, aren't I?

I'M MODERN and I run a modern business. We're linked up around the world. We sell in 42 countries. So I'm aware that from a practical point of view, we need to be *modern*, but from every other point of view, I'm purposely trying *not* to be fashionable.

I THINK THE big change is that the designer label is not really a designer label anymore. Of course

"Some of the future generations may actually reject the fact that everything is so specific and corporate."

there are lots that are, but generally speaking, they are brands, they're not designer labels. When I started out, the key point was individuality, getting something in your head, putting it down on paper and hoping somebody liked it. Now it's all, 'Ralph is in black, so you must do black'. Or 'So and so is doing this, and you must do that'. 'They're spending that much on advertising, so we must spend that much on advertising.' 'They're on Bond Street, so we must be on Bond Street.' It's the lack of individuality which is anathema to design, because design is about an idea. These days, it's not about an idea any more, it's about marketing.

BUT I'M an odd person from that point of view. I think the most important factor for my business is that I own the company with Pauline, my lady; we own 85 per cent of the company, and the remaining 15 per cent belongs to our finance guy who's been with us for a long time. So we've got no shareholders breathing down our necks saying, 'More and more profit, more expansion.' I had a conversation with somebody recently, who had found out that we have sales amounting to £177m. That person said to me, 'I never realised your company was that big because it's got such a small company feeling about it.' Which is *fantastic* to hear, because that's exactly what I would hope someone would say.

I'M PURPOSELY TRYING not to be cookie-cuttered, not to just churn out clothes. We even work hard at designing clothes that don't have a particular identity at all. We do use our logo sometimes, but very little. It's my one major battle with my staff, *not* using the logo. And often when you see T-shirts with Paul Smith on it, they're copies. We've got 120 cases of fraud at the moment just because we don't use our logo. Youth culture has always demonstrated that the next generation don't want what Dad had. So if you can make your clothes fairly 'non', without the logo everywhere, then you've probably got a longer future.

I THINK ONE of the ways forward is to understand that some of the future generations may actually reject the fact that everything is so specific and corporate. There will be people in society who might be 11 now, who have already been in a nice car and eaten at a nice restaurant, perhaps seen death or childbirth live on the Internet. By the time they get to 18 or 19, they'll go, 'Well, I've done that. I've done the moon ... now what?' I'm hoping that people will want something called 'normality'. That can be something simple, like somebody asking how you are and actually being interested in how you are. And I play lovely tricks with people. When they say, 'How are you?' I say, 'Actually, I've got a really bad back.' They say, 'Oh good, pleased to hear that.' And if you say it in a certain way, when you're at a petrol station or something, it's a fantastic ruse.

THAT KIND OF superficial behaviour is awful. I can see a future of mergers everywhere, which I think

Giorgio Armani
Launched in 1973, Giorgio Armani's talent and entrepreneurial spirit are two qualities which have enabled him to establish a fashion empire with estimated sales of over $1 billion. Building a brand around his unique vision, Armani has developed a style which eliminates the superfluous, emphasises the comfortable and stresses the elegance of the essential; his approach to fashion is timeless and yet always timely. Over the years, Armani has launched a number of other brands including Emporio Armani, clothes for a younger customer marketed under the distinctive eagle logo, and fragrance brands such as Giò and Acqua di Giò.

GIORGIO ARMANI

"Anybody who can duck and dive and appeal to human beings in an individual way will do really well in the future."

is a dreadful thing, personally. Maybe it will benefit the consumer in terms of prices going down, but it'll almost certainly create blandness, nothingness. And I do think that goosebumps and tingles in your tummy and things that make you feel special are going to be so valuable in the future, because there'll be nothing else left. I mean, I think for the 11 year-olds of today I just mentioned, the only thing that will make them feel very special is falling in love or having a baby, you know, the fundamentals. Because everything else will have been done. Tick … done that, done that, done that. Horrible.

MY BEST-CASE VIEW of society would be one in which the large corporations put back into society in some way or another, and some of them do that already. Business has to be a catalyst for some big changes, otherwise the world will explode. It could be charitable donations, or bosses setting standards of morality, or putting an element of their very large profits into promoting young designers. Whatever it is, they're putting something back. And ultimately, trying to keep competitiveness alive amongst young people, but without making young people feel embarrassed if they aren't successful in a clichéd way. Because I think success can be the fact that you have a craft in your hand. You might only earn £10,000 a year, but you might be a brilliant stonemason, or you might be a charity worker. I think at the moment we're all so locked into the fact that we're supposed to have a phone, a credit card, a Porsche, a mortgage; we seem to have lost touch with things that come from the heart.

I THINK PEOPLE are more fashionable now, and more interested in nice interiors and nice meals. As we become more susceptible to stress and pollution and climate change, then presumably we'll be looking for some sort of medication to keep us young and beautiful; that kind of brand will be important. But hopefully, if future generations don't just get watered down and beaten over the head by mediocrity, there might be a few rebels out there who say, 'Actually, I'd like some fish and chips in a paper.' Or, 'I don't care, I'm going to wear my Dad's old clothes and that's it.' There will be an element of rebelliousness there that will make life a bit more interesting, because after all, the only thing that's left for us human beings is us. Everything is so advanced now, and the only thing left is: 'I like you, you don't like me.' 'I've got a cold, I haven't got a cold.' 'I'm moody, I'm not moody.' 'I'm attractive, I'm not attractive.' So anybody who can duck and dive and appeal to human beings in an individual way will do really well in the future."

Coca-Cola®

Coca-Cola must be one of the most universally recognised brands. Its distinctive bottle shape and red and white logo are now familiar in more than 195 countries. Coke has come a long way from its origins in an Atlanta drugstore, but its basic promise has never changed: great tasting and refreshing. Coca-Cola is a classic brand which has been managed in a meticulous fashion over the years. Despite the encroachment of own-label in its mature markets, the Coke promise remains appealing and relevant; it will be interesting to see how the brand copes with the challenges of the next 25 years.

"I'm only a kid, but my hope for the future is that people can get their priorities better sorted and lead less stressful lives."

Thomas Carr is not only one of the hottest surfers in the UK, he and his surfboard are tipped for international fame, and all this aged just 15. Since he learnt to surf at the age of 12, he's won a number of competitions and in 1998 he became the Grunta Junior Champion. English and History are his best subjects at school and he hopes to study sports science at university. During the weekends and school holidays, all year round, Thomas can be found surfing on the beautiful beaches near his home in Woolacombe, North Devon.

"WHEN YOU ASK me what a brand is, it's a difficult question for me to understand. But if you ask me to name some brands, I understand exactly what you mean! I think a brand is a name and a logo attached to a product; it's used mostly in advertising and sponsorship to promote that product.

THE BRANDS THAT I'm most interested in at the moment are surfing brands, because surfing is what I'm most interested in, full stop! I've been surfing for about 3 years now, and I love it, it's excellent, really good fun. You can be outdoors in the sea at any time of year, having a great laugh and meeting loads of people who are really cool. My favourite brand is probably Kangaroo Poo, because they're my sponsors. They're very good to me and they give me free clothes. Even if they weren't my sponsors, they're nice clothes anyway, so I'd still wear them. Or else it would probably be one of the bigger surf brands, like Quiksilver, or Billabong, or O'Neill. Outside surfing, my favourite brand is probably Jaguar, because me and my Dad are always very impressed when they feature Jaguar on *Top Gear*.

LOTS OF BRANDS seem to be trying to get involved with surfing at the moment, and I think it's because it's become quite a fashionable thing. If you go to London or other big cities, you can see these huge brand stores like O'Neill, and you wonder how many of the people who shop there have even seen the sea, let alone actually tried surfing. I'm not really interested in fashion. There are some people in my class who take it really seriously, they have to wear the right stuff or else. Nike and Adidas are two of their brands, but I don't like wearing them because it's like being a slave. You look around and you see everyone wearing the same symbol. I don't like that because it's like following the herd.

SURFING DEFINITELY isn't a fashion thing for me; I've been competing in local competitions for approximately a year and a half. I won a competition which was sponsored by Coca-Cola and I thought at the time that that was a bit weird. For me, there has to be a clear link between the brand and the person or the event they're sponsoring. I mean, it's nice to come out of the water and have a can of Coke, because it's fizzy and it gives you an energy boost, but what's the relationship between Coke and surfing? It doesn't make much sense to me. I won a board which had the Coke logo on it; it was a good board but the logo put me off a bit. It's not a proper surf logo, really, and so I was advised to sell it. I was told it would be really popular with tourists, but for me, it just wasn't authentic. Still, I guess that for Coke they wanted to get more involved with the coolness of surfing, and it was certainly good that they helped make the competition happen. A much better example of good sponsorship, I think, is when Playstation sponsored the first local surfing competition at night. In my mind, there's a good fit between them, because of all the lights and special effects.

SPONSORING THE best people is one of the most important ways of showing what a good brand

"You look around and you see everyone wearing the same symbol. I don't like that because it's like following the herd."

you are. I mean, when I think of Quiksilver, I immediately think of Kelly Slater, who's six times World Champion. Quiksilver sponsor the best surfers in the world, and so you know that they're the best because you see the guys in magazines surfing their boards and wearing their clothes when they win competitions. I guess that's why Kangaroo Poo want to sponsor me, although I'm nowhere near as good as Kelly Slater! I suppose they like to see their name appear in local papers when I'm featured for winning competitions. They're not half as well known as the other surf brands, so this is better than taking out a newspaper ad to sell their products. It's the same with other brands. During France '98, Nike had those adverts on TV with Ronaldo and the rest of the Brazilian football team on the beach, and you just know that Nike are the best, because Ronaldo is one of the best football players in the world.

I THINK TV advertising is really important for brands. I think it's a good way of getting the message across, especially if the adverts are interesting or they keep you in suspense. Sometimes you're wondering what they're trying to prove or what they're trying to sell and then the Nike logo flashes up and it all makes sense. But if it's something mundane like washing up liquid, then the advert's all very nice, but it seems a bit disappointing. I suppose it's because I'm not really old enough to care about the washing up!

ONCE YOU'VE SEEN a brand on TV and then you see it in the shop, it does make you more likely to buy it, because you know it's good. Like with camera film; you see Kodak advertised on TV and then go into Boots and you buy Kodak because you remember the advert and you don't recognise the other brands on the shelf. That's what usually happens, except where food is concerned; the burgers never look as good when they're given to you in the paper cartons as when you see them on TV! My burgers always end up much smaller, with a single piece of lettuce and half a strip of cheese. Stick with Cornish pasties! But there aren't really any particular pasty brands I can think of, not like fast food brands such as McDonald's and Burger King. Perhaps that's an opportunity for the next few years?

IN GENERAL, I think things should actually get better in the future. I mean, take the example of schools. Twenty-five years ago teachers were allowed to hit kids but now general attitudes to children have become more relaxed, lenient even, compared to 'You should be seen and not heard'. So I think in 25 years, the old rules could be bent even further. I think that technology will develop quite a lot and I definitely think fashion will change. If you think about 25 years ago, you had people wearing big flares and stuff, and now people are starting to wear flares again. It could be space suits in 25 years, you never know.

I THINK Disney will still be a great brand in the future, because they seem to keep getting bigger with

Kangaroo Poo

The last decade has seen Kangaroo Poo grow from a small surfer-run company, producing surf wax and T-shirts, to a respected international brand stocked by over 500 retailers. Whether on the mountain or beach, street or sidewalk, Kangaroo Poo now fulfils the needs of sideways surfers globally. New ranges are being developed all the time by a core team of designers, with valuable input from sponsored athletes such as Thomas Carr, in order to extend the appeal of the distinctive Kangaroo Poo style.

"Sponsoring the best people is one of the most important ways of showing what a good brand you are."

their new theme parks. Also, they bring out new cartoons every year, which then give rise to toys and other products which keep the cartoons alive. If little kids think of one of their favourite cartoon characters, it will usually be a Disney character. So if you tie in little kids now, in 25 years, when they're grown up and they're asked 'What's your favourite cartoon character?', they'll say the same one, like Mickey Mouse or the Little Mermaid; they'll want their own kids to like that character, too. I guess McDonald's will still be quite big, but there's all sorts of other fast food places around as well, like Burger King. McDonald's is a well-known one, but the food isn't much different from its competitors; it's just a quickie meal, just a burger or something. So I'm not so sure people will specifically choose McDonald's over others in the future.

FOR MYSELF, I'm not really sure what I'll be doing in 25 years' time. Hopefully it'll be something to do with surfing. Or maybe outdoor pursuits in general; I don't like the idea of being in an office all day I wouldn't mind designing logos, actually, that would be quite fun! My personal word for the future would probably be ambition or something like that. There are lots of things I want to try and do, like travel a lot more. I'll know what I'm doing as a job, without being too old to stop doing things. And another word would be life, 'cos it's going to be the main part of my life. If I get married and have kids and stuff it's probably going to happen in the next 25 years.

IF I COULD invent anything in the whole world for the future, it would probably be a wave machine for use in cities, because a lot more people could then get a chance to try surfing, and they'd love it. And it would make me a lot of money, because city surfers would pay to use it! I think more people in the future should get involved with surfing because of what it offers in terms of relaxing and chilling out; physical exercise and enjoyment and just putting the worries of the day behind you. I'm only a kid but it seems to me that adults are always really stressed, and my hope for the future is that people can get their priorities better sorted and lead less stressful lives. But that's easy for me to say, because I don't have any responsibilities!"

McDonald's

Dick and Mac McDonald opened the very first McDonald's in San Bernadino, California. But it was Ray Kroc who developed the concept into the brand we know today – the world's largest food service company. Now, the famous 'Golden Arches' are a familiar sight in 115 countries around the world, and the business continues to be committed to the brand's key attributes – Quality, Service, Cleanliness and Value. The key to McDonald's success is its ability to meet consumer needs consistently, but in a way that is relevant to the local culture.

"Team sport is very important today and will be in the future, because the family no longer plays the role it should play."

Sepp Blatter is President of FIFA, elected to the ultimate role in international football in 1998. An active footballer for over 20 years, his professional career started in tourism before he became General Secretary of the Swiss Ice Hockey Federation. He acquired his first taste of the international sports scene at Longines where he was involved in organising the 1972 and 1976 Olympic Games. He joined FIFA in 1975 and was promoted to General Secretary in 1982 and to Chief Executive Officer in 1990. A total of 5 World Cups have been staged under his auspices.

"FOR ME, brands have always been synonymous with quality. That's something I learned in my childhood. My father was a working man and we weren't rich, but he always said, 'A good brand name means good quality. It's better to pay a higher price and to have a good product.' Brands guarantee a sense of quality, of reliability, and they give you a sense of good feeling, of dreams – that's why people buy brands. The first brands that I remember are Palmolive, Lux and Colgate. In fact, I still use Colgate toothpaste today. In a world where so much is changing, where families are no longer as strong as they were, where there is often insecurity and lack of respect, brands are things that people can trust.

ON A PERSONAL LEVEL I'm still very 'branded' – I like good clothes, I like watches, I like cars. I'm attracted to high level brands; Longine and Patek Philippe are both wonderful. I identify with brands which are linked to dreams of mine. I used to have dreams of good clothes – something I never had when I was young. Another of my dreams was to have a comfortable car. Now I drive a small Mercedes – the big Mercedes is too big for me.

SINCE I've worked in sport, I've come to admire 2 brands in particular – Adidas and Coca-Cola. I especially admire Adidas' consistent use of the 3 stripes. If you see 3 stripes on any piece of clothing anywhere, you identify it with Adidas, even if it isn't Adidas. Coke I think is the best known brand in the world. I've always liked their approach. I like the colour, I like the design and I like the product. Everyone recognises Coke and Adidas, and they've worked very hard for a long time to achieve this.

WHEN I STARTED to work in football, I realised that nothing had been done on branding. Even today we're still limping behind American sports organisations like the NBA, because for so long nobody realised that there was a market in football beyond equipment. Some of the football clubs are beginning to pick up this brand understanding – Manchester United, Juventus, Inter Milan. Bayern Munich is one of the leading football brands right now; I know that they hired McKinsey to advise them. For most clubs, the value of the brand is still linked with the success of the team. That's why I believe it's important to develop the FIFA brand. When Bayern Munich and Real Madrid start to lose, somebody else will replace them. But FIFA will always be there.

FOOTBALL is such a wonderful game. It provides spectacular entertainment but it also has a great educational role. As the governing body, we should have attached more importance to the FIFA brand. It's not too late now, because it's never too late. But it's our last chance to get it right. I want FIFA to stand for joy, for hope, for education, for respect, for entertainment. That's what we have to work on. My vision for 25 years' time is that a team like Bayern or Liverpool will use their brand in

"I identify with brands which are linked to dreams of mine."

connection with the FIFA brand, because FIFA will stand for quality, for fair play, for model ethical values. They'll still sell their products at a club level, but they'll use the FIFA brand to say, 'We are from that family'. That's a vision, but it's also a conviction. I'm *convinced* we can do it, but it needs time and effort and exposure.

FIFA HAS A wider role to play in world football. Professional football only accounts for 0.25 per cent of the players in the world. All the others are amateurs and 80 per cent are youth players. So the FIFA brand needs to stand for education – for self-discipline and respect for others and team sport. Team sport is very important today and will be in the future, because the family no longer plays the role it should play. Human beings want to live in a community and football is the best sport of all for this. Why? Because everybody can participate, whether they're tall or small, fat or thin. Everybody. Girls and boys. You're never alone and it's easy to play; you only have to kick a little ball into a net. You learn to fight, because it's a contact game, but you learn to fight fair. You learn to win, but you also learn to lose. So the FIFA brand stands for joy, hope, respect, fair play, strengthening of character, and it will be a great achievement to communicate that. At the same time, FIFA has a vital role to play in the drama of world class football. The football stadium is the biggest theatre in the world. There are 300 million active participants in football. And if their families are buying things for them, that makes 1.2 billion people. One fifth of the world's population. So the FIFA brand has an opportunity to participate not just in education and entertainment, but in the welfare of society. We can help people achieve a better understanding through the medium of football. That's why I believe in the FIFA brand.

IF I HAVE A WORRY, it's that some entrepreneur might come along and try to take away the best of football and make a circus out of it. You know, forget about its educational role, and the importance of the different national associations. I fear interference by businesses or television, trying to arrange the game so that it fits in with their schedules. I think it's vital that the game remains the same all over the world. We can't have one game for professionals, and one game for amateurs. The other danger is political interference. The European Union is suggesting that anyone can play anywhere. The essence of football should be the club. So in your city, in your region, you have a local identity, and as a nation you have your national team, your national identity. Commercial or political interference would be detrimental not only to football, but also to society. You would be taking away the best of football from regions where football gives so much hope – Africa, Asia, the Caribbean. FIFA stands for the whole family and if part of the family goes away, then it's over.

ALL COMMERCIAL brands want higher profits, but every company knows that they must have a social or cultural 'package'. Over the next 25 years, brands will need to move away from the so-called

FIFA

FIFA (Fédération Internationale de Football Association) is the world's governing body for football. Founded in 1904, it has overseen the growth of football as the world's most popular sport. Over the last 25 years in particular, FIFA has encouraged the development of the game in regions such as Africa and Asia, including the award of the 2002 FIFA World Cup to Korea and Japan. Indeed, under FIFA football can truly be said to have become a universal language, understood by people everywhere. Committed to the values of respect and fair play, FIFA is now determined to help lead football into the next millennium, as the world's greatest game.

"The hope, the aspiration of any human being is to get something of more value."

American profit thing. We need a new approach to close the gap between the work of rich people and the work of poor people. If you think only about profits, the gap between rich and poor will continue to widen. We're lucky at FIFA because our message is already cultural. Football is already about people coming together. Our product is not a ball, it's not a shirt, it's not something you can eat or drink. It's this game called football.

IT'S DIFFICULT to make prophecies about which brands will still be great in 25 years' time. When Benetton first came onto the market, I didn't think it would get anywhere, because I couldn't *feel* a Benetton product. And now Benetton is a worldwide brand, though I'm not sure they'll still be strong in 25 years. Adidas will still be here, *definitely*. Nike's another strong brand, even though they're only 25 years old. The other brands that will still exist even if you try to kill them are cigarette brands like Marlboro, because people will always smoke. Even if cigarette advertising is banned here, in other continents smoking has just become fashionable. It's a question of personal choice.

CNN IS ANOTHER brand that I think will last the distance. It's an information channel and information is what people want. People aren't really interested in technology, they're interested in what technology can bring them. We'll be able to access CNN via our televisions and our mobile phones; we'll take CNN everywhere. You'll still be able to buy some newspapers, but people will prefer to access news through their mobile phones. They'll have no time to read a big paper. I'm not sure the Microsoft brand will survive because it's about technology, not the end benefit. IT development is still in its childhood, and as it grows up, other brands will emerge.

I THINK FIFA will still be here in 25 years, if we take good care of football. My hope for FIFA and football is that the game remains the universal game with the human face and that through our brand we can transmit the message of hope and joy. One thing is certain, brands will still be important in 25 years' time. Forty years of communism tried to suppress all private initiative, all personal identity. And it didn't work. The hope, the aspiration of any human being is to get something of more value. Brands represent aspiration, dreams. I was in Nigeria during the World Youth Championship and Coca-Cola was distributing little bottles of Coke to people. It was tremendous to see how they reacted. It was a symbol to them, a symbol of their aspiration. And it's true – the more you achieve, the more you want. It's the same all over the world."

Colgate

Colgate began as a soap, candles and cheese business in Manhattan in 1806. In 1873 it produced its first toothpaste in jars, and since then the Colgate name has become synonymous with oral hygiene products. The latest addition to the Colgate range is Colgate Total, the only toothpaste to receive the prestigious endorsement of the FDA for its ability to help prevent gingivitis, plaque and cavities. Colgate has strengthened its leadership in the oral hygiene category with a number of cause-related marketing activities, most notably the Bright Smiles, Bright Futures Volunteer Partnership in the US.

33

"Don't use the branding word, do the actions!"

Rita Karakas is President of RSKarakas Associates Inc, and works as a consultant specialising in organisational development and strategic change management within the NGO sector. Rita's early experience was gained in the community healthcare field, where she worked in Montreal with organisations such as the Ministry of Health. In 1984 she was appointed Vice President of United Way/Centraid Canada and then took up the post of Chief Executive of the YWCA of Canada. In 1991, she was appointed the first Director/Creative Head of TV Ontario. Rita currently sits on the Boards of the Canadian Human Rights Foundation and Greenshield Canada.

"I HAVE TWO understandings of brand; one is a differentiating strategy which is probably marketing led, the other is more organic: it's an essential description of how you know yourself to be, how you wish yourself to be and how you want yourself to be understood. I have been involved with 4 major branding projects during my career, and I've seen them from very different places within each organisation. My own role in each project has conditioned my understanding of what a brand is, and how this definition has evolved over recent years. Two projects required the repositioning of an entire institution, the YWCA and TV Ontario respectively. And in both instances, branding was used to differentiate, to attract new audiences, whilst retaining some continuity with the past. With the YWCA, for instance, that meant turning around a non-image conscious organisation with 17 logos in just one country!

THOSE EXAMPLES I think of as 'classical' branding projects. The other area I'm familiar with is the branding of public awareness campaigns, and that involves understanding the subtleties of branding a concept, rather than a simple product. 'Participaction' was an attempt to get public awareness for fitness in Canada; labelled it, designed a logo and then advertised the heck out of it! Whereas 'Imagine' was a campaign which helped Canadians to understand the distinction between charity and philanthropy and then persuaded corporations to give 2 per cent pre-tax profits as charitable donations; it was very subtle, very slow, and it took over 2 years to launch the brand.

I USED TO SEE a real difference in approach between the 2 sectors, but that difference is merging. The notion of having a vision, a purpose, organisational values which are embodied in the culture, that's being increasingly adopted by the private sector. And in the voluntary sector, the notion of being more professional and cost-effective is taking root. Everyone knows that you no longer simply sell a product, you've got to hit the heart. But it's important to remember that the heart is not just on the outside; you need the insiders to carry on feeding that heart.

THAT'S WHAT we're building on here, here being Oxfam, where I'm currently a consultant. We're introducing branding into this organisation because of its international affiliation; the public just can't understand why during an emergency there are 10 different Oxfams with 12 different T-shirts running around. So in one sense, this is a marketing strategy. But what I'm really interested in is helping the organisation come to terms with how it actually owns branding as an attitude, as a presence, as a state of mind, a *politique de presence*; where everyone is a communicator and everyone is an embodiment of the essence of the organisation. The challenge is to ensure that it's not artificial, it's not just 'Here's the manual, this is how we've got to do it'. The brand must come alive because it's interactive, it's not a static logo which you change again 10 years from now.

"It's important to remember that the heart is not just on the outside; you need the insiders to carry on feeding that heart."

THAT'S WHERE BRANDING as a discipline will have to evolve in the future. If organisational development and branding are seen as 2 separate strands, what happens is that the branding activity often loses out to the predominant culture, to cynicism, lack of ownership. So my approach is 'Don't use the branding word, do the actions!'. Don't focus on training which dictates 'This is how you use it, this is how you don't use it', focus on 'This is why we've done this and this is how you can personally contribute'. Otherwise it's like some customer service training, it's artificially implanted. You can actually hear the training, it hasn't been assimilated.

THERE ARE CERTAIN brands which I think have really managed to integrate themselves as part of their organisational culture; they've avoided this potential clash between their branding and their corporate culture. For example, I was due to fly Business Class with Virgin Atlantic; I didn't really know what to expect, but it was everything you hoped the brand would deliver. What was really wonderful about it was that it took you right back to what travel should be about – it was fun! You could even get a manicure on board, and you didn't feel silly and pretentious doing it. CNN is another great example, although being a Canadian, I hate to admit it! It's such an American experience, it's a profound culture in itself and that's what it's selling. It's selling the US view of events and its penetration over such a short space of time has been remarkable.

ANOTHER BRAND I have always admired is Coca-Cola, for their profound, complete capturing of a lifestyle. Yes they've made mistakes in introducing products like Classic Coke, but they've always regained their position. It will be interesting to see what Coke do next, because in many parts of the world the aspirations inherent in their brand have been met. And by that I don't mean what you can buy. I mean what you can look to, what information there is about the world, what's now within your reach. From a personal perspective, I'd also mention Duracell, Levi's (I like them because they have a good donation policy!) and Johnson & Johnson: safe, secure, responsible – I like their products.

I THINK IN THE FUTURE, aspiration is going to take on a different meaning, smaller groups will have more focused aspirations. Demographics will help to predict the behaviour of these groups in the future, and a key sociological trend to watch is the elimination of childhood and the 'third age'. How old do you have to be to be old now? 70? It used to be 65. How old are you when you're a child? 8? It used to be 12. I think we will see a lot of brands emerging in the 'third age' sector, perhaps a great brand of the future will be a retirement complex! Exclusivity is a key to aspiration; access is not. But it's interesting, you have to have sufficient access so that you can continue to aspire. How does the lottery work? Somebody has to win for you to keep buying your ticket. I think in the future, aspiration is going to be about uniqueness and diversity, completely the opposite of a blanket approach. I was in Istanbul recently and I'm looking around, thinking 'Why don't I like it? Why am I not comfortable? It

Johnson & Johnson

Selling products in more than 175 countries, Johnson & Johnson is the world's most comprehensive and broadly-based manufacturer of health care products and related services for the consumer, pharmaceutical and professional markets. A caring and trustworthy brand synonymous to many with mother and baby products, at a corporate level Johnson & Johnson has more than 188 operating companies and owns a range of household names such as Tylenol and Band-Aid. Founded in 1876, the brand still operates according to its founder's enlightened Credo which lists its responsibilities in order of importance: customers first, followed by employees, community and stockholders.

Johnson & Johnson

"The branding challenge for the future is to maintain uniformity so that the brand centre is whole, but promote diversity and uniqueness at the tip."

doesn't feel like Istanbul any more.'. And there's a KFC, a McDonald's, a Wendy's. I'm not sure that McDonald's will be around in 25 years for that reason, people will want something distinctive, not ubiquitous. Here's the key branding challenge for the future: maintain uniformity so that the brand centre is whole, but promote diversity and uniqueness at the tip.

TWENTY-FIVE YEARS AGO in the West, we all predicted that we would have more leisure time. We don't. We are simply living more healthily and living longer. This makes community and family even more important to us, though the definition of family has clearly shifted; many families now are non-linear in the sense that they don't share the same DNA, and I think that makes them very strong. However, many of us are also living poorer in many ways: morally, financially, health wise. So when I think of major issues in the future I worry about lack of community. After all, community is as much about exclusivity as about inclusivity – what's going to happen to refugees? Is there going to be a fortress Europe? Or is there going to be a beneficial blending of populations? I worry very deeply about racism, not specifically in the West, but in Kosovo and Rwanda. We haven't yet come to terms with how we handle large bodies of people. And we must, because the world has become smaller, there's no place to throw them where people can't see them anymore. Technology, transportation, CNN and the Internet, they're all converging; we don't have 'out of sight, out of mind'. When you wake up one morning and see people walking up the beach of Newfoundland and they're Sri Lankan refugees, you know it's absolutely one world.

MANY PEOPLE expect the voluntary sector to solve these problems, to provide the balance of power in the future; I don't. If you want to find out about an NGO, don't listen to its voice, look at who's funding it. Most international NGOs are an expression of state pride. The more liberal the society, the more likely the existence of a state instrument for aid and development. So many NGOs become a vehicle for the privatisation of state aid under the guise of democracy. The International Red Cross is the one NGO I would point to which is currently a universal brand and which should still be one in 25 years' time. It has an absolutely consistent visual identity which has both a local and an international meaning for individuals; you can get blood from the Red Cross at your local hospital, and you can see their work as a vital part of international agreements. Hopefully Oxfam will be another, if we can succeed in answering questions such as 'How does Oxfam reflect me? Who exactly am I affiliating myself with? Which larger community is this making me a part of?'. It's about winning hearts and minds. Because, after all, what is Oxfam? What's the 'product'? The 'product' is affinity, the 'product' is change for the better."

Oxfam
The Oxford Committee for Famine Relief was set up in 1942 to highlight the humanitarian problems caused by the Allies' naval blockade of Greece. Today, Oxfam International comprises a group of independent, non-governmental organisations dedicated to fighting poverty and related injustice; these affiliates include Community Aid Abroad in Australia, Intermon in Spain and Novib in the Netherlands. In order to create maximum impact through its work, Oxfam International has developed a common logo and word-mark which will be introduced around the world; in a fresh and distinctive green, it comprises the 'O' and 'X' of Oxfam which form the shape of a human being.

"In developing markets, you can see a backlash against the equation of everything Western with a good life."

Geoff Lamb is Director of Trust Funds and Co-financing at the World Bank in Washington. Born in South Africa where he was a journalist (and subsequent political prisoner), he undertook postgraduate studies and then became a Fellow and Deputy Director of the Institute of Development Studies at Sussex University. Geoff joined the World Bank in 1980 and literally worked all over the world before heading a group working on the transition countries of the former Soviet Union, Eastern Europe and the Middle East. Prior to his post in Washington, Geoff was head of the World Bank's office in London.

"I THINK WE ARE entering an era of enormous growth in corporate global linkages and power. The branding and identifying of corporations is both a symbol of that, and one of the engines behind the process. Along with that growth of corporate reach, however, we will also start to see the vulnerability of corporations which don't respond to their stakeholders' interests – and respond in ways somewhat akin to governments. The corporate governance experience in recent years is that, if you're big enough, people start to go after you as if you're a government. If you're a big corporation, you're going to have to respond to a whole range of interests as well as your shareholders. You're really going to need a public position on all these issues to defend your brand. Corporations will have to pay much more attention to things like human rights, labour standards, environmental standards, what you might call 'fair trade'. That, I think, is going to become a much more important requirement. If you look at the experience of, let's say, Nike, over the whole labour standards issue, or Shell in Nigeria, that was hugely significant for them. In other words, the more companies become globally powerful, the more brands become political.

IN MY rather naive view, a brand is an *identifier* for a stream of goods or services, and it evokes a fairly powerful set of messages to the consumer. I guess the greatest brands for me are the ones that resonate particularly about information, about values that are global, challenging, high quality – the ones that represent the leading edge of what could change things in the world. And oddly enough, that makes rather traditional-sounding brands like The Financial Times, the BBC, very potent for me. They represent freedom of information, but they also represent intellectual challenge and a demanding discourse. They make a certain kind of demand on the consumer, rather than merely satisfying some pre-existing 'want', and communicate a definite positioning about quality, reliability, challenge.

IF YOU LOOK at the developing nations, or the former Soviet Union, what is striking is that the global or Western brands that became most rapidly established were those which were very aspirational. You know, they were to do with modernity, Westernism, the new availability of information that had previously been prohibited. From a personal point of view, the brands that became very prominent then were not ones that I would choose as the best symbols of the new world: they were fast food and cigarette brands! But they were the things that symbolised what people aspired to. You saw a similar thing in East Asia a few years ago, where Remy Martin or Courvoisier sometimes seemed a symbol of everything that the prosperous new East Asian middle classes were aspiring to. Interestingly, in Africa, a couple of brands have become very much part of local culture. For example, Guinness is strongly associated with sexual potency. And there's this Swahili ad in East Africa that's been going for years which shows a very healthy, virile-looking bloke and the slogan is just 'Guinness is Power'. And the kind of power being discussed is pretty obvious, from the context!

"The bad news for developing countries is that we're using less and less of what they produce."

IN SOME developing markets, you can begin to see some kind of backlash against the equation of everything Western with a good life. It is interesting to speculate whether that push-back against the received Western model will be transformed into an identification with domestic or non-Western brands – I don't see that yet. It's more at the political and ideological level, where people may be saying, 'These Westerners are subverting our teenagers and trying to make us adopt their values'. But the kids might be wearing branded sneakers while taking part in demonstrations against Western domination. So the new global political economy is full of ironies and contradictions.

IF THERE'S A SINGLE WORD I would use to describe the future of brands, it is 'convergence'. If you look at the brands in the world today, they're not signifying the same things they were some time ago: they're less and less about bashing large bits of material into shape. Until recently, brands have been stamps of identity on *things* – motorcars, sneakers, watches, toothpaste. But if you think of the next 25 years, the transformation of electronic communications means that *things* will be less important. I suspect that a lot of future brand activity is going to be around communication-based convergence. It's going to be brands which are about information, financial transactions, travel, mobility, services. And less about disparate families of products or things. That's what I mean by convergence.

ALAN GREENSPAN, the head of the US Federal Reserve Board, said a very interesting thing. Although US gross national product in value terms is now many multiples of what it was 100 years ago, it probably *weighs* about the same. In other words, we've gone from an economy which bashed a lot of metal and produced a lot of heavy goods, like locomotives, machines, huge buildings, to an economy which produces far more in value, but much less stuff – i.e. things which weigh less, and use fewer materials, and are much more service-intensive. The cell phones that we use probably weigh a tenth of what phones weighed 15 years ago. But the real value of the services which now come down that phone is many times greater.

THE BAD NEWS in this for developing countries is that we're using less and less of what they produce. We're using less copper, less steel, fewer tropical crops to make rope or sacks – and we can only drink a finite amount of tea or coffee, the espresso boom notwithstanding. So poor countries are stuck for the most part in the production of what the rest of the world needs less of. Guess what happens to their income, unless they can diversify fast? In terms of brand building, the real problem for developing countries, including the ones that have become most successful, is how they go the Japanese route: how to transform their equivalent of Honda from a little putt-putt, two-stroke bike into a symbol of quality and success, into a really powerful brand. That I think is something that most of them have not cracked yet.

"The more you can bring countries into the mainstream, the more everyone benefits."

FOR ME, the worst-case vision of the future is what I would call a two-track world. You would have one world in which countries are involved in a global economy and interact more and more with each other – travel, trade, investment, culture, foreign exchange. And then there'd be a marginalised 'other world' of the poorest countries that would be pretty much cut out of the mainstream of human civilisation. It may sound pompous, but I think that it's a real risk, particularly if you add in some of the negative global forces like Aids, which is a huge and potentially crippling development problem, reaching pandemic proportions in many poor countries. It would make a very insecure world, and a world in which personal values might become much more selfishly defensive. Much more 'Let's keep them out' or 'Let's protect our own' or 'Let's put higher walls around what we've got'. And that doesn't seem to me to be a very attractive world to live in. The opposite of that, the best case, is that the more you can bring countries into the mainstream, the more everyone benefits. And our sense of life is broader and more hopeful. I think that remains true despite the wobbles of globalisation – like the Asian crisis of 1997/8 – and despite the great social inequities which can result as countries join the mainstream, and some groups in society make out much better than others.

IF I HAD TO PREDICT which of today's brands might still be great in 25 years' time, I suppose I would pick those that are about information and about health. I think that what people are going to want to do is to manage a whole lot of information about their lives, and they're going to be worrying about health, longevity, replacement parts. I'm not so certain that many of the great brands of today are going to be that big in 25 years, because I think other sorts of business will have overtaken them. For example, if Yahoo! remains a winner in cyberspace, Yahoo! may become much bigger than McDonald's; you can only eat so many hamburgers but our demand for information is, in principle, infinite. And even if the Chinese are eating hamburgers as well, the Chinese are also going to be using the Internet. So I think relative positions will shift a lot.

IF YOU WERE to push me to invest my money right now with a view to 2025, I'd probably take a deep breath and look for the next Indian 'killer' software company. Out there somewhere around Bangalore, there is potentially some small company that is developing what the computer nerds would call a killer application – the next big thing in electronic communications that we would all love to own a piece of. But the difference – going back to 'convergence' – is that our mythical start-up is going, somehow, to crack the cybernetics/biology divide, and that's what will really make my heirs rich. I would love to say that the company that discovers a vaccine for malaria will make a lot of money. I know it will do a huge amount of good, but I'm less convinced of its financial potential. Still, I hope they discover it all the same."

BBC

The BBC has been a major international brand since 1922. It was founded by John Reith who coined the mission statement still used today: 'Educate, inform and entertain'. He predicted the value of the logo, branding everything from microphones to vehicles, and built a temple to programme making with the BBC Broadcasting House in London. In the 1990s, with digital beckoning and broadcasting going multi-media and interactive, the BBC has strengthened and empowered its logo. The award-winning solution has reclaimed the brand through creative design and strategic marketing, communicating the value delivered to audiences through the licence fee.

"The good opinion of the public will become increasingly important to big brand owners. If you've got a message, it has to have some truth in it or you'll be found out."

Steve Jones is Britain's best-known geneticist. Professor of Genetics at the Galton Laboratory at University College London, Steve was co-editor of the *Cambridge Encyclopaedia of Human Evolution* and joint author of *Genetics for Beginners* and the Open University's final year genetics textbook. Following his acclaimed BBC Reith Lectures in 1991, his book *The Language of Genes* won the Rhône-Poulenc prize for best science book of 1993; his second book *In the Blood*, published in 1996, coincided with his BBC TV series. Steve presents *Blue Skies* on BBC Radio 3.

"ONE OF THE common misconceptions about the future is that there's going to be a genetics revolution, like the industrial revolution, and the world will change. There isn't and it won't. However, genetics is certainly in the culture; it is finding its way into mainstream marketing. BMW has used DNA sequences in its advertising, and I appeared in another car ad! The science will certainly make a difference at the margins, and will revolutionise things like cancer treatment, but beyond that things will be pretty much the same. I don't even think that life expectancy will increase all that much. If we're being realistic, if you look at the developed world and you take into account things like infectious disease, starvation, cold, smoking, alcohol and air pollution, we've probably made most of the advances we're going to make. What's happened is that we've won the battle against the enemy outside. What we've got to face now is the enemy within, which is our own inborn weaknesses. I'd be very surprised if medicine is as successful in dealing with the internal enemies, basically decay, as it has been with the external ones. So I would like to think that we're *already* living in utopia or on the threshold of utopia; which might seem a bit depressing given the state of the world today – but would seem a perfectly fair statement to someone transported to today from Shakespeare's time.

IF YOU WANT TO look for a revolutionising force in society over the next 25 years, I'd say 'homogenisation'. In fact, world homogeneity is most emphatically here already. I was in South Africa recently and I was struck by how much more homogeneous society had become in the few years since I was last there. You see it everywhere. Brands are clearly responsible for a lot of this homogenisation, though I don't think it's all positive. In countries like South Africa, brands like McDonald's are causing major changes in people's eating habits. I've really noticed a lot more obesity there, and this seems to be as a result of the belief that this American kind of diet is the right thing to have. Still, I don't blame McDonald's. I don't expect any corporation to have a real social conscience because that's not what they're for. If a corporation's social conscience stops it doing business, then it ceases to be a corporation

LET'S TAKE GM foods. People go around moaning and beating their chests about Monsanto. What's Monsanto for? Monsanto is a company, it makes profits for its shareholders, and it has to do that with new technology. Now, it's arguable that some of that new technology could be damaging – in fact I think some of it may well be. But you can't blame Monsanto for that fact. Monsanto is using the technology as much as it's allowed to, in the same way as during the industrial revolution, people polluted the atmosphere of Britain because they were allowed to do so. It's up to either public pressure or governmental pressure to make them stop. So the good opinion of the public will become increasingly important to big brand owners. You only have to say the name Monsanto now, and so many people say 'Boo!' So, something has gone terribly wrong. Whereas in fact, what they're doing is not much more than what lots of other people are doing. The irony is that in my view, GM

"I guess I don't really think about brands all that much, but now you mention it, I'm using brands every day of my life."

food is perfectly safe. I'd far rather eat GM foods than I would the American diet, the 'fast food' diet. In that sense you can't blame cigarette companies either, because they're doing what they're allowed to. Education doesn't seem to be stopping the spread of smoking, so the only way to control cigarette companies is government action. How successful this will be, I simply don't know.

AS AN INTERNATIONAL traveller, what I appreciate most about brands is that they guarantee consistency. It's a relief (even if it's not very romantic) when you're travelling to be able to rely on something being the same all over the world. I don't drink Coca-Cola – in fact I've never had a Coke in my life – but if you buy a Coke anywhere in the world, it's always a Coke. Consistency is also what I appreciate about Holiday Inn. For somebody who travels all over the world as I do, working in places that are quite uncomfortable and sometimes, to be honest, dangerous, to walk into a Holiday Inn is just a complete pleasure. It's always the same; it's clean, it's safe, you're not being hassled, and that's a great plus. Swissair is another good, consistent brand and they've given me really good service when I've flown with them. I admire their attention to detail; they even provided me with a spare pair of trousers when the passenger next to me was sick!

I GUESS I DON'T really think about brands all that much, but now you mention it, I'm using brands every day of my life. You know, I go to Sainsburys, I use Kodak film, I've got a Sony television – though I bought it in 1970 – I wear Levi's, I used to own a Mercedes truck. My favourite brand is Guinness, but that's really because it's one of my favourite products. When I was a lad, I used to drink a lot of Guinness. I like the taste. It's predictable, like all great brands. The trouble with bitter is that it varies, you don't know what you're going to get. So far none of the companies that specialise in genetics have become strong brands. There are quite a few biotech companies with rather strange names out there. There's Genomix and Biotech and Decode Corporation. And they're all promising something rather vague. In fact, much of what they sell their stock on is their trademark. Rather than anything they have actually achieved. In the early days investors saw some sexy name like Genomix and said, 'Oh, that sounds really good'. Investors didn't really understand what they were promising and a lot of them have got burned. If you've got a message, it has to have some truth in it or you'll soon be found out.

ON THE OTHER HAND, many of the biggest corporate brands in Britain are the extremely profitable pharmaceutical companies. Ironically, though they're putting enormous quantities of money into genetics research, billions and billions of pounds, their profits still come from the conventional blockbuster drugs. Perhaps there will be a gene-related brand in the future, but it's not here yet. Of course, genetic manipulation can already be found in some of the world's leading food brands. I think this whole debate about GM foods has focused on the wrong things. I often say that we've

Swissair

The national carrier of Switzerland came into being in 1931. Its red and white identity is still closely based on the Swiss flag. Today, the airline has a worldwide reputation for fine service, outstanding quality and excellent customer care, and has won many awards. Swissair flies a young fleet and is highly aware of its environmental responsibilities. Indeed, it carries out regular environmental audits and recently became the first airline to introduce organic products into all classes.

"If you want to look for a revolutionising force in society over the next 25 years, I'd say 'homogenisation'."

basically messed with biology 3 times since the war. And we've got away with it, just, in 2 of them. The first of them is antibiotics. Penicillin came in 1942. In 1944, if you'd stood amongst a bunch of doctors and said, 'Look, by the year 2000, we will only have one antibiotic left – all the others will be useless', everybody would have looked at you as if you were mad. Well, that's what happened. And it may well be that medicine's finest days are over, because there are no more antibiotics. And all those bacteria which can easily kill you will just come back.

IF YOU LOOK back now from the perspective of 1999 at the way we used antibiotics, the way we're still using antibiotics, all you can say is it was criminal lunacy. We must have been insane. We must still be insane to spray antibiotics onto fruit trees to get 1 per cent increase in yield. We're still doing it. We must be mad. If you look at insecticide resistance, again, it's exactly the same story. Crops like cotton are being given up in many parts of the world because they have to spray them so often to let them grow. Because of agricultural spraying, malaria mosquitoes have become resistant to insecticides. So, again, malaria's come back. We thought we'd won – we've lost. In South Africa, in the last 2 years, they've lost 50 years' progress in terms of the spread of malaria. Now, with genetic manipulation, we've got a technology which is much more powerful. Should we be using it as we used antibiotics, as we used insecticides, for the first and most obvious thing, which is to grow a bit more food? In my view, absolutely not. We should say, 'This is a fantastic piece of technology, let's just use it for the most precious things of all'. So, for example, we should be growing vaccines inside bananas in carefully controlled conditions in greenhouses. If pressure isn't put on major corporations, we might not get away with it for a third time. The risk is small, but the damage could be disastrous."

Monsanto

The life-sciences company Monsanto is dedicated to finding solutions to the global need for food and health. Founded in 1901 in St Louis, Missouri (still the group's global headquarters), the company now employs 30,000 people internationally. In 1982, scientists at Monsanto became the first in the world to genetically modify a plant cell; since then, Monsanto's gene technology has been responsible for producing, among other things, the world's first genetically modified soya bean. The principles of sustainable development underlie much of Monsanto's current business activity. NutraSweet, the aspartame sweetener, and Roundup, the herbicide, are among the company's best-known brands.

"The responsibility of our brand
is to make a positive contribution
to changes in people's lives."

San Jin Park is Vice President of Global Marketing Operations at Samsung Electronics in Seoul, Korea. A graduate of Seoul National University, he began his career in the AV division of Samsung Electronics where he was responsible for the Overseas Strategy Team. In 1992 he moved to Europe, working initially as President of the German business; he was then promoted to become President of the French Business and in 1996 he was promoted to the role of President of both the Spanish and Portuguese businesses. He was appointed to his current position in 1999.

"I THINK A BRAND is an embodiment of the comprehensive promise made by the company to the outside world. It's a proposition of the value provided to consumers by the company, and it's all the underlying corporate activities that support that proposition. All these constitute the brand. In my opinion, the most prominent brand in the world today is Microsoft. With the introduction of its new operating system, Microsoft brought about a complete change in the way we use computers, thereby playing a huge role in transforming the lifestyle of mankind. On a smaller scale, I think Singapore Airlines is probably the greatest brand in Asia. When you think of Singapore Airlines, you associate it with a high-quality, premium image; it's a brand of high esteem, and I think it's a very successful brand in that respect. My personal favourite brand is Sony. (Actually, this is a company that we at Samsung Electronics are competing against both directly and indirectly!) The thing I regard most highly about the Sony brand is that it has always maintained a consistent image of uniqueness. With this 'uniqueness' as its corporate slogan, Sony has always made great efforts to keep its brand promise, and even though there are bound to be some differences in various parts of the globe, Sony continues to maintain an image that is virtually identical all over the world. And by keeping pace with the speed of technological development and maintaining consistency in its brand statement, Sony continues to offer an image of uniqueness and innovation.

IN TERMS OF food brands, my favourite is McDonald's. I particularly admire this brand because it provides quality assurance; you will always get the same value for money even though it operates in many different countries using the local ingredients of those different places. It's also a great brand in that by marketing to the younger generation, it ensures that wherever they are, those children will grow up and still enjoy eating hamburgers even after they have children of their own.

OBVIOUSLY I THINK of Samsung as a great brand. I think the responsibility of our brand is to make a positive contribution to changes in people's lives, and at the same time, make profits as a company and provide a stable livelihood for our employees. On a national level, as the leading brand of Korea, the Samsung brand should contribute to the promotion of our country's image, while also meeting the needs of customers and contributing to their fun and leisure activities. What's important for all brands is to keep apace with changes in lifestyle. Going too fast is no good either. One has to perceive the signs of change and meet the needs of the new trends.

I THINK the recent developments of digital technology, and in particular the explosive growth of the Internet will bring sweeping changes to the world in the future. Digital technology enabled the production of computers, and evolved with the development of PCs. However, it was only with the emergence of the Internet that those gradual alterations gave way to the major transformations that are taking place on an explosive scale, bringing about fundamental changes to our lifestyle and

"Since people can't touch and feel the things they are looking for on the Internet, their dependency on brands will increase greatly."

behaviour. I think the future development of digital technology will cause our physical life to blend with the virtual world, leading to lifestyles that we have never experienced before. For example, the scenes in science-fiction movies depicting virtual reality may one day become a reality for us! And as the increased use of the Internet shopping mall illustrates, digital technology is already bringing changes to almost every aspect of our lifestyle, which is a real benefit. But at the same time, this means that any company that fails to keep pace with these sweeping changes may be heading for a terrible nightmare; the inability to build up the value of a corporate brand in line with such trends may threaten its very existence.

LET ME ELABORATE on how the significance of digital technology can be explained in a historical context. Looking back, one can see that every superpower in history emerged from a 'road' or 'route' of some kind. First, there was the Pax Romana, a period in which the Romans tried to pave the way for a homogenous Europe by building roads for people to walk on. Also, when Genghis Khan unified Mongolia's northern plains, roads were made to connect the East and the West for travel on horses; this opened the door for cultural exchanges between the two regions. Then, following the opening of ports in the 15th and 16th centuries, there was the time of Pax Britannica, when Britain gained hegemony by connecting the sea–land routes. By the same token, the United States, the first country to introduce the concept of highways, is currently pushing ahead with the construction of the information super highway. And the driving force behind this is digital technology, which is paving the way for the construction of the super highway in the virtual world, which in turn is linked with the Internet, which we use in our everyday lives. So the 'information super highway', based on digital technology, creates a new 'route' for us, one that combines the physical world with the virtual. And I think this will bring about massive changes in our lives over the next 25 years that are barely imaginable at this point.

HOW THIS WILL IMPACT upon the future of brands is a very difficult question. I think brands will change in line with the other changes in our lives; take shopping, for example. Up to now, people went to a certain place to shop; they had to touch and feel the product before making a purchase. But in the future, I think the online shopping mall will absorb most of those shoppers, provided that there is little difference in the quality of the products sold online, and this means that shopping around will not really be necessary. Of course, people will still want to shop in the real world for things that are directly related to their personal taste or sensitivities. But by and large, cyberspace is where most shopping activities will take place in the future, and where most sales will be recorded. And since people can't touch and feel the things they are looking for on the Internet, their dependency on brands will greatly increase. So, with this increased importance of brands, I think the key challenge for all corporations in the future will be to find ways to enhance the value offered by

Sony

This multinational corporation was founded in Japan in 1946. Consistently at the forefront of innovative technology, Sony has led the field in the home entertainment market, introducing the world to the home video system, CD player, camcorder, Walkman and most recently the Playstation, which has enjoyed worldwide success. With such a strong brand name and clear values, the company has moved easily into the wider entertainment world, acquiring both record labels and film companies. Sony has achieved the ultimate brand accolade with the adoption of 'Walkman' as the generic term for personal stereo.

SONY

"The most prominent brands in the future will be those which build networks."

their brands, so as to secure the deeper trust of their consumers. And I believe that the most prominent brands in the future will be those which build networks. This is an area that has a direct influence on our lifestyle. First, home networking enabled the connection of all homes with the outside world via the communications network, and now mobile networking is bringing new changes to our lives by connecting the personal appliances carried by individuals with the home network or other networks.

THIS MAY SOUND ironic, but I believe that even though it's important to develop state-of-the-art technology, focusing too much on technology alone may undermine a company's efforts altogether. We have to remember that in the world of technology, keeping ahead of the others is a great advantage, but the same technology that helped us advance may prove to be our worst enemy if we take a single wrong step. To prevent this from happening, and for a great brand to remain great after 25 years, the brand's activities need to offer consistent value under a consistent corporate philosophy. And in this respect, I think the GE brand is a good example. Despite changes in the contents of its business, GE has always maintained this consistency, and will probably still be big in 25 years' time. Another example would be Sony, as I've mentioned. However, I'm not sure what the future holds for Microsoft; they must keep vigilant and continue to seek positive changes. This is especially true when considering the flood of cheaper PCs targeted at the general public, rather than the experts.

ANOTHER SECTOR that I think holds great potential is bio-engineering, or genetic engineering. Despite the controversy surrounding this industry, it is another area that can bring huge changes to the life of mankind. It's true that people currently feel uncomfortable about the idea of genetically manipulated food, but if the technology proves its safety, governments will give the go-ahead for their widespread production and people will be more inclined to accept the whole concept; more importantly, it may provide the fundamental solution to the global shortage of food. In the United States, the jump in Monsanto's stock prices despite the social controversy over genetic manipulation is proof that it's becoming a very powerful brand.

THIS YEAR MARKS the 30th anniversary of Samsung, and it makes one wonder how the Samsung brand will be perceived another three decades from now. As I said, in order to survive in the electronics field, we have to develop hi-technology, but what is just as important, or even more important, is to select the path that we will follow, because we can't own all the technologies in the world; I think we will probably become more strongly linked with the service and contents sectors as well. It's a question of corporate philosophy or brand value. We have to figure out the best way to keep our brand promise for our customers."

General Electric

Consistency is the hallmark of General Electric and the GE Monogram. The millennium marks the 100th anniversary of the company's famous trademark, the unifying symbol behind one of the world's largest, diverse and most successful companies, begun in 1878 by noted inventor, Thomas Edison. The GE Monogram can be found around the world on a wide range of consumer products including lighting, home appliances and financial services, and industrial products like jet engines, medical imaging, motors, power systems and information and financial services. GE operates in over 100 countries and employs nearly 300,000 people worldwide.

"Many brands have forgotten about taking risks, it's no longer part of their way of thinking."

Patrick Gournay was appointed Chief Executive Officer of The Body Shop in 1998, following a 26-year career with Groupe Danone in France, Italy and the USA. Initially in an organisational development role, he soon progressed in sales and marketing to become Vice President for Sales and Distribution for Gervais Danone. In 1989 he became President of Danone Italy and was then appointed President of the Danone Company in the USA; in 1997 he was promoted to Executive Vice President of the North and South American Division of Danone where he was responsible for managing 8 companies in 5 countries.

"FOR ME A BRAND REPRESENTS a contract between the consumer and the company. It's a symbol and promise of a definable quality and experience that the brand guarantees the consumer. A great brand is more than just a great product; a great brand is something that people want to be part of and share in, a way of expressing themselves. There has to be something about it that differentiates it, and makes it interesting and exciting and attractive to consumers. Such a brand can also help the consumer make choices, particularly in markets that are becoming increasingly crowded; it makes decisions easier for the consumer.

A BRAND that represents these qualities for me is CNN. CNN is definitely my brand of choice when I turn on the TV looking for news. I look for CNN, and I know I can get it wherever I am in the world. Two brands illustrating the confidence and trust that are a key component of a brand are Sony and Gillette. Each represents that quality of standards and experience in its field that I know is right for me. In electronic goods, I'd also include Bang and Olufsen, although there is a somewhat mistaken perception that their products are too expensive. Having these brands around means I don't have to think too much – these brands help me with choices. I also know that these brands are concerned with innovation, and that they will always have the latest and best products – they are at the cutting edge.

BRANDS WILL INCREASINGLY have social significance. There is a distinction to be made between brands that are merely good corporate citizens – whose social activity increases their standing with consumers and results in a commercial payback – and brands that have stated beliefs and are not afraid to stand up for them. It's not just about corporate citizenship and good business sense. It is also about being genuinely driven by consumers and their changing attitudes. In Germany, consumers actively reject supermarket goods that they believe are over-packaged. While this is an extreme reaction you do not find currently in the UK or the USA, it will happen increasingly in the future. Consumers are looking behind the brands, at what the company is like and how it acts in the round.

THE BODY SHOP will continue to promote cruelty-free products, but we are pushing hard into the broader territory of ethical sourcing. We are moving beyond personal products to a more holistic approach to well-being. And we are about more than natural products; there are plenty of natural products around, and lots of retailers and brands have their own natural product ranges. Increasingly, The Body Shop will leverage wisdom and knowledge from local cultures into good products for our consumers. It is our ability to access and use and celebrate this knowledge that makes us different, and this will be important to us in the future.

SUCH LOCAL KNOWLEDGE is essential to us because we are simultaneously global and local. The Body Shop is a global brand, but we haven't lost touch with consumers at the local level. It's difficult

"I think it's very difficult for an active manager of a large business to be a spokesperson for social change at the same time; it takes a lot of courage and there is definitely a price to pay."

Lynne Franks founded one of the UK's leading consumer PR companies when she was 21. She soon had Europe 'Swatched', revolutionised young men's attitude to Brylcreem and put British Fashion Week on the international calendar. Twenty years on she sold the company to focus her communications expertise on encouraging partnerships between business and society. Lynne is currently developing Globalfusion, a virtual training network with an emphasis on sustainable enterprise. She has also recently launched Lynne Franks LA, a consultancy connecting people, ideas, businesses and institutions.

"WHAT'S MY DEFINITION of branding? Well, I suppose we've had branding in some basic sense ever since Adam and Eve, in that God was the label used for divine energy. People have always needed labels like brands, but you could say that Christianity was the first real world brand; and of course, it's not just a label, it's about identity and belonging. Marketers know that people need to identify with something and that's how labels such as Coca Cola and Kellogg's have become brands, by building up these kinds of strong relationships with their customers. To me, the most important recent shift in branding is that consumers now understand that this relationship is a two-way dialogue; they make their own demands on brands, and these demands, combined with new ways of interactive communication, will shape the future of branding.

INTERACTIVE TELEVISION and the digital world are going to make a huge difference but I don't think that anyone's really started to think about how. There's an extraordinary opportunity. If one thinks about the power of interactive television, one of the most powerful business people in the world over the next 25 years will be Rupert Murdoch, but I don't think he has a real single brand yet – that's his mistake. And of course in contrast there's Bill Gates who has consolidated his position in a single brand, Microsoft. The future of the world is inextricably connected with computers, and so Bill Gates hasn't just got brand power, he's got actual power. From a global perspective, I'm sure that CNN will also be a great brand of the future; CNN was the first to catch onto the whole area of global news, and when you're the first, on that scale, you can stay in that position for a long, long time.

FOR ME, THE CLEVEREST piece of brand marketing in the last few years has been the resurrection of Apple. The campaign posters feature incredibly interesting photographs of incredibly interesting people with a different take on the world, famous icons such as Yoko and John and Leonard Bernstein, and they really help to communicate the brand's vision: 'Think different'. The iMac is brilliant. It's a great product in its own right, but from a branding point of view it's a perfect example of vision fulfilment; it really does demonstrate different thinking in the sector, and sales in Macintosh have gone through the roof because of it. The key to this success is that Apple have absolutely understood whom they're selling to, they know their market. People who buy a Macintosh want to be different. They want to be creative and be seen to be creative. Again, it's all to do with that sense of identification with a brand. 'Do I want to be that woman in the Kellogg's ad?' 'Well, actually I don't, personally. I'd rather be Yoko Ono in that Apple ad.' Apple's audience want to be individuals. And certainly all over California and New York Apple is everywhere now. They've put their money into these enormous billboards and building sites, inspiring everyone with the brand's message. They use a tiny little Apple icon and the phrase 'Think different'; it's confident and works so well. They're doing a very, very good job.

"The most important recent shift in branding is that consumers now understand that the relationship is a two-way dialogue."

IN A GENERAL SENSE, if you look at the way society is going, you can see how brands will have to change in order to survive. My vision of the future is polarised. On the one hand there's global overpopulation and the 'Coca-Colarisation' of indigenous people, and on the other hand there's a move away from globalisation and a return to such things as community life, small businesses, respect for the individual; it's a return to real values. I hope for balance. If we're not careful, the way we're going, there will be more aggression, more destructive tabloid journalism, more moral dilemmas for us all. But at the same time, there will be a growth in personal responsibility. For brands, this means developing real integrity; brands will be destroyed if they have anything to hide. A brand will have to represent values that actually affect people's lives in a positive way. This ties in with the current shift towards cause-related business practices. Or rather, socially responsible business practices; the term 'cause-related' marketing can already be seen by some to be just one more gimmicky marketing ploy. It's a sad fact, but now I'm in California, I can see that the 'non-profit' world in the US has become very big business, with all the moral compromises that can bring.

NOW THAT I'M living in California, in many ways I feel that I'm seeing the future right before my eyes. California is definitely way ahead. I am personally very attached to Trader Joe's, a brand which has real integrity; it's probably the best food retailer I've ever come across. It's a small chain with 90 odd stores, mostly in California. They sell healthy organic food, but much cheaper than other retailers, and most of what they sell is their own brand – vitamins, everything. They even do their own packaging. Anybody with real intelligence here shops at Trader Joe's. It's mainly food for single people and busy people, but it's totally healthy, and because it's so obviously appealing to a particular lifestyle out here they don't have to do very much advertising. They just do a little bit of radio advertising, and some community PR. The Trader Joe's idea could certainly expand world-wide. In fact, they could be the top supermarket in the world one day, I reckon, certainly targeting the younger market, anyway.

TAKING THE wider view, Trader Joe's will be a great brand of the future, because the company takes real responsibility for the products it sells. Taking responsibility for how your products are produced will increasingly become part of sound business thinking – look at how Nike's brand credibility has suffered because of the bad press about the way some of their shoes were produced. The way you do business really does relate to the strength of your brand. And this could be a problem for old style FMCG businesses, they're often still stuck in the old bureaucracies which don't readily allow for this responsibility. And that's why I believe cigarette brands have really had it – how responsible are they? Marlboro now feels so old-fashioned. To me, the Marlboro man is a dying man.

AVEDA IS ANOTHER brand which I believe will go from strength to strength, just so long as it doesn't get 'corporatised' by Estée Lauder. The founder, Horst Rechelbacher, realised that the amount of

Trader Joe's

Trader Joe's is a privately held California-based chain of value priced speciality food and beverage stores with 120 locations in California, Arizona, Nevada, Oregon, Washington, Massachusetts, New York, Connecticut, New Jersey, Maryland and Virginia. At Trader Joe's, the product mix is a combination of ongoing items under the Trader Joe's label and specially purchased items. The mix is constantly changing and this helps Trader Joe's to offer a fun and intriguing food shopping experience. Buyers travel to Europe, South America and Asia several times a year searching out unique products. In addition, buyers make special purchases of interesting foods which are presented throughout the year. Every item must pass the company's tasting panel, and thousands of items are tasted each year.

TRADER JOE'S

"Taking responsibility for how your products are produced will increasingly become part of sound business thinking."

'stuff' that goes on women's faces and bodies can be really damaging if the wrong ingredients are used. It's not just about not testing on animals, it's about not testing on humans either. I've seen Horst Rechelbacher stand up and address all the potential health hazards for women that the cosmetics industry often tries to ignore. In general, though, I think it's very difficult for an active manager of a large business to be a spokesperson for social change at the same time; it takes a lot of courage and there is definitely a price to pay.

WHICH NEW BRAND today do I think will be great in 25 years' time? Of course I'd like to see my own brand up there, which I'm launching next year! It's called SEED, Sustainable Enterprise and Empowerment Dynamics. SEED is a 12-week training programme to help women empower themselves to start up their own small businesses; it's all about creating a business in a feminine way, using training and networking and a series of books. This can be for any type of business, and I'm hoping to include women from developing countries who have their own craft businesses and so on. Obviously I think it's going to be enormous! In many ways, I feel I'm selling a sense of belonging to something big, and I'm selling to many types of women the power and the reassurance that goes with that sense of belonging. These values will be underpinned by the brand's identity, which will use metaphors of planting and growth and bloom – a real sense of life and hope and success for all.

I GUESS in the final analysis, you can divide current brands into three categories. Are you a brand that was established recently with the future in mind? Or are you a brand which is trading on your heritage, but with the future in mind? Or are you just living off your heritage without really thinking about the future at all? For me, a company like Kellogg's is in danger of falling into the latter category. However, Levi's is a good example of a company with heritage that is changing the way it does business – for example, its research into organic cotton. Visa is a great example of a business of the future which was founded 30 years ago. In fact I'd say Visa is also one of the top brands of today, even more than many computer brands. We are moving into a cashless society, so the basic core of the brand is fundamentally geared for the 21st century."

Visa
Visa is the world's leading financial services brand with 800 million cardholders worldwide and global sales of nearly $1.4 trillion. Visa currently processes up to 2,400 authorisations per second and by 2000 this is estimated to rise to 17 billion authorisations per year worldwide. Visa is the closest thing to a universal currency and the brand's declared aim is to replace traditional cash and cheques as preferred forms of payment. To further this aim and to extend the reach of plastic, Visa Cash, an electronic alternative to cash, was launched in 1995, and Visa is also pioneering SET Secure Electronic Transaction™ programs for payment on the Internet.

"One of the reasons the Internet has become so popular is that people have this buried hunger to re-connect."

Kyle Shannon is Chief Creative Officer of AGENCY.COM, an electronic media consultancy he co-founded in 1995. Working in advertising in the early 90s, his interest in technology led him to discover the nascent World Wide Web. Recognising its potential as a tool for creative expression, he launched Urban Designs, one of the first online venues for art and culture and soon after he founded the World Wide Web Artists Consortium. By challenging people to think beyond established boundaries, Kyle is constantly seeking to find new interactive solutions that maximise the possibilities of the online medium.

"THE GREATEST BRAND IN THE WORLD for me is Apple, and to take that a step further, the combination of Apple and Steve Jobs. People are brands as much as companies are brands, and one of the most powerful brands moving into the 21st century is the brand of the individual. When I grew up, I got my first computer in 7th grade, a TRS-80. That was the time when Steve Jobs and Bill Gates were on the covers of magazines as the founders of the PC revolution. I always envied Steve, being in the garage with Wozniak soldering together logic boards and knowing something that no-one else knew. I have always had a place in my heart for Apple because it was born from that initial spark. Steve's return to Apple has shown how quickly he can have an impact on the brand and the brand on him. I think the combination of Apple and Steve Jobs is one of the most powerful brand stories that I know.

THE MICROSOFT/BILL GATES relationship is also fascinating. For the first 2 years of the Internet revolution, Microsoft said 'It's not about the Internet, it's about our proprietary network called MSN'. Then enough people whispered in Bill Gates' ear and he stood up at a conference and said 'Proprietary networks are dead. This is about the Internet and Microsoft is about the Internet'. Before that event I didn't think it was possible for a large brand to shift its focus so quickly. And with Bill's statement, Microsoft truly turned on a dime. But I think that Microsoft has still got some brand image problems. At the moment, they are one of the most vilified brands out there. Thank goodness their competitive strategy is solid.;-)

IF YOU LOOK BENEATH the Microsoft brand, some of the values they represent are frightening. My worst-case vision of society is that people listen to Bill Gates' 12 rules for the digital future, and they use technology to separate themselves from society. I mean, one of his rules is that all communication should be relegated to e-mail, which I fundamentally disagree with. Technology is simply a tool, it's not the ultimate replacement of human interaction. If we, as a society, get seduced by technology (or the brands who are profiting from it) and think it's about us connecting with the technology, we have a very bleak future indeed, very Mad Max.

HOWEVER, if we use technology to connect *with one another*, things will be quite remarkable. One of the reasons the Internet has become so popular is that people have this buried hunger to re-connect. For the past 50 years or so, television, radio and magazines have told us who we should respect, who we should vilify and what issues are important. But they have pushed us farther away from one another. So it makes sense that the first media technology which allows people to connect on a global scale is a runaway success. The Internet allows us to re-connect with each other in very powerful ways. For example, a 5-year-old who grows up all of his or her life with the network won't have the concept of division between cultures and societies. So when that 5-year-old is 15 or 20,

"One of my beliefs is that it's not about technology, it's about how you use technology."

wow! What a connected brain they're going to have! The kind of interactions they demand will fundamentally change the rules of business and society. The backlash has already started and will accelerate, forcing companies to lead, follow or get out of the way.

ONE OF MY BELIEFS is that it's not about technology, it's about how you use technology. A lot of executives in Silicon Valley are wondering where the magic went. It almost seems as though people don't care if you double the clock speed of that Pentium chip anymore…well, guess what…they don't! Back to Apple and Steve Jobs. The release of the iMac series of computers marks a very significant shift in the PC industry. A whole new breed of people bought an iMac because it was their favourite colour rather than the fact that there was amazing technology under the hood. The challenge facing technology companies is making that transition from 'more technology is better' to 'what service is also needed?' I think that Dell has made that transition very well. Dell realises that it's not about machines. It's about customer service. They developed their customer support infrastructure so that the individual could use it directly. They made it so that the web-site knows the individual machine you bought and what the problem could be. Sure, someone else might have a more powerful machine or a better price, but customer peace of mind is where Dell derives its power.

THE ROLE OF ELECTRONIC MEDIA in society is that it should disappear. You shouldn't even notice that you're 'going to the Internet'. It should just be there, with what you want, when you want it. Electronic media should be part of the fabric of the way we communicate. It's not a thing we go to. It's not an event. You don't log on. We're not users. We aren't viewing pages. None of that. It's just there. If we call something a 'page' on the Internet, we're going to *design* pages; we're going to think about how to deliver print media in a new place. If we look at the Internet and only see what is behind us, we will miss its real power, which is the fact that it's experiential and participatory. Online, brands are immersive. Like a good theme park, you can actually enter the brand, explore it and relate to it on your terms. So, how do you enter a Hershey bar? Well, if you go to Hershey, Pennsylvania, you drive down the street, it smells like chocolate. You see Hershey Kiss street maps. You ride the rides. You enter the brand. What I'd like to see is that as an industry we're not fooled into thinking that we've got it figured out. So much has been written about the Internet, people feel like they understand it: 'We put left hand navigation here. We put content in the middle.' Just look at the evolution of the film industry. When film was invented, you paid a penny in your local drug store to watch someone sneeze over and over again. It was 26 years before the release of *Birth of a Nation*, before DW Griffith figured out that if you edit some of those shots together you could tell a story. Look at the Internet right now. It's not very compelling. The brand experiences are dreadful. We spend a lot of time looking at people sneezing. And I don't know that we've got a DW Griffith yet. It's probably one of those 5-year-olds out there who lives and breathes the network.

Dell

Dell Computer Corporation is the world's leading direct computer systems company and the fastest growing among all major computer companies. Dell sells customised desktop and notebook computers, workstations, network servers, storage products and related software and peripherals, increasingly via the Internet, to businesses of all sizes, government departments, educational institutions and individuals. The company also provides an extensive range of value-added services, such as leasing, system installation and management, 24-hour technical support and planning and execution for technology transitions. Dell operates under a simple philosophy that guides everything it does: Be Direct.

"A brand used to be a promise but as we move forward, a brand is a relationship, a living thing."

A BRAND used to be a promise but as we move forward, a brand is a relationship, a living thing. It's no longer about 'company knows best, we're the company, we make up the rules and you live by them'. What existing brands and new brands are going to have to do is get back to the *relationship* word, to really listen to customers and have the courage to respond. They might say 'We can't give you that, go somewhere else'. At least it's better than not saying anything, or making promises and not delivering them. You can't say 'We're faster' and not be faster, because people will find you out.

IF AMAZON KEEP ON doing what they're doing, I think they're going to be around for a while. In the future, they might not even sell anything tangible. They might be the next AT&T. Because what they're really about is connecting people and AT&T is about connecting people. If it's not about technology, it's about the quality and nature of the relationship, so maybe the Amazon brand is about relationships and maybe they'll be known for that rather than selling books. Other brands that could be great in 25 years' time are the brands of the individual. Companies will be rewarded if they stop treating mass-markets as mass-markets and instead treat individuals as brands. It's very cyclical isn't it? Individuals who gain power because of their own brands have their own brand equity and their own life-time value; those individuals that develop better relationships and learn to leverage their individual brand will potentially become very powerful brands themselves. It used to be important to be tied to an existing brand; being a Steve Jobs tied to an Apple. But now with the Internet, each individual has a brand and has brand equity.

EVERY INDIVIDUAL a company ever touches is equally valuable. It used to be that there were the 'power customers', and the rest of us; not any more. If you leverage people's individual brand power, you'll be rewarded, and if you don't, you'll see your customers flowing out the back door faster than you can imagine. Schwab's killer application is an interesting story. Apparently their goal in 1997 was to shift 50 per cent of their trades online; once they did that, they were going to close down their least-profitable stores. So they shifted 50 per cent of their trades online and then had to open 200 additional retail centres. Because it just floated the boat. It made existing customers trade more. It created new customers who wanted to come to the store. It was about relationships, not technology. For me, the future of brands is the future of relationships."

Schwab

Charles Schwab & Co Inc was founded in the early 70s as a pioneer discount broker; its aim was to empower individual investors. Schwab has always had a reputation for innovation, so it was no surprise that it became the first major US financial services company to offer trading via the Internet. Within a week, 10,000 customers had signed up. Now, Schwab serves over 5 million investors around the world and technology is seen as the enabler of all that it does. Indeed, Schwab has been described as a financial services company on the outside, but a technology company on the inside.

Charles Schwab

"We're not interested in a world in which there are no differences, in which everything is brought down to the lowest common denominator."

Sir Michael Perry is Chairman of Centrica plc, Chairman of Dunlop Slazenger Group, Deputy Chairman of Bass plc and a non-executive director of Marks & Spencer plc. He is also Chairman of the Marketing Council, Chairman of the Shakespeare Globe Trust and President of the Liverpool School of Tropical Medicine. After 39 years with Unilever, Sir Michael retired as Chairman in 1996. His career included periods abroad and he served as Chairman of subsidiaries in Thailand, Argentina and Japan. He received his knighthood in recognition of his services to industry and export in 1994.

"I THINK THE future for brands is very bright. The same principles that always applied still apply. Brands in the future will need to continue to be totally customer-focused. They've got to be carefully crafted and they've got to be competitive. We're not interested in a world in which there are no differences, in which everything is brought down to the lowest common denominator. We glorify the differences, and as consumers, we pick out those differences which appeal to us personally. The brands that we are associated with are expressions of us and that will always be so, whether it's wearing a fine fragrance or buying gas. Brands help to fulfil us, and the brand owner's skill lies entirely in continuing to stay ahead of competition. So it's a constantly evolving, dynamic, iterative process, out of which can come only one thing – progress. The only thing that can stop that progress and the acceleration of that progress is some kind of artificial interruption of the process of free trade. Progress in this area is about the freedom to innovate and to keep on saying to people, 'What about this new idea? Have you seen this new thing that I've just made? What about this new service I've just designed?' And that will never stop.

I THINK SHRINKING geography, shrinking distances, will be a determining factor in the future development of brands. It's been happening for a long time, in every sense, and is already transforming everything we do. It will make an enormous difference to service provision, for example. There's no longer any reason why electricity used in any home anywhere in the world should not be generated anywhere else. The old boundaries of national borders are making way for a different kind of demarcation, a different kind of market definition, which is quite separate from national political boundaries.

STILL, the essence of what a brand is has not changed very much over the last 25 years – a unique combination of functional, emotional, rational and irrational benefits and qualities. What have changed are the criteria for what constitutes a brand. I often quote the example of the original branding of a bar of soap – what the brand did then was to bring into play concepts of quality, predictability and consistency which hitherto had been absent. Now manufacturers have to go beyond those simple statements, meaning that brands have become much more sophisticated, much more complex. A bottle of Calvin Klein perfume now elicits a whole wealth of different consumer responses, all of which are carefully engineered by brand owners and which in total give rise to the perception of the brand.

I THINK it's very hard to pick out just one or two brands as the world's greatest. One admires certain brands over time which have consistently succeeded in adapting themselves to the changing needs of their own generation. Some of these have of course achieved immortality in a way. Coca-Cola undoubtedly is in that group and Kellogg's and Heinz … and there are many others.

"The brands that will be big in the future will be those that tap into the social changes that are taking place."

MY PERSONAL favourite brand is, I think, the Morgan car. It's a brand I'm very happy to be associated with. I haven't always had Morgan cars, but at times I've had two. Now I have one and it's all I can do to fit into it, frankly, but I do so with great pleasure. I don't know that the brand necessarily reflects me. What it does do is give me a great bounce and a feeling of stepping into the past, of being part of a long, now almost dead tradition of privately owned car building in the UK. I think Morgan's about the last survivor. And I find it very satisfying to be part of that ongoing and continuing *small* but *real* success.

I ADMIRE Virgin, a brand that isn't now linked to any product category at all. The Virgin brand is a mixture of intangibles; wrapped into it are elements of quality, elements of value, elements of price, elements of the personality of the founder. As a result it's more stretchable and more transferable across category sectors than certain other brands. Another great corporate brand is Microsoft. Microsoft has captured the imagination of the world by a mixture of extraordinary inventiveness, great entrepreneurial skill and an ability to stay out in front which is unmatched. If you measure those things in terms of corporate results or the wealth of the individuals responsible, then everything is there in fairytale terms for Microsoft.

INTERESTINGLY, both the Virgin and Microsoft brands are inextricably linked in the public perception to their founders. The personality of Virgin is totally linked to the personality of Richard Branson, just as the perception of Microsoft is totally linked to the personality of Bill Gates. As a result, these companies appear to be extremely dependent on the skills of one person. I think that this inevitably makes their sustainability more doubtful, more at risk, than some of the other big corporates. I couldn't name all the geniuses who have run Coca-Cola over the years, and in the case of Procter & Gamble, nobody quite knows who Mr Procter or Mr Gamble might be anymore. And the same would apply to all the great Unilever brands or other major houses which are much more concerned with groups and teams of people.

THE BRANDS that will be big in the future will be those that tap into the social changes that are taking place. At the moment we can only guess at some of the changes to our patterns of life. Look at McDonald's. We think of McDonald's as having been there forever. But in fact it's relatively new and has flourished in response to a particular set of social changes which gave rise to the need for a predictable, reliable source of fulfilment. People don't have big family meals at home anymore. Mostly, people graze individually. A few years ago, the average family meal took 2 or 3 hours to prepare. Right now, it's down to 15 minutes and that's because we use more and more stuff which is brought in. This concept of 'bringing in' is, I think, going to turn the whole distribution system upside down over the next period of time. In some ways things will have come full circle. When I was a boy people used to deliver

Virgin
Richard Branson's Virgin brand is one of the most dynamic brands in the world. It began life as a mail order operation in 1970, but is now one of the most diversified brands in the UK. The Virgin name appears not only on record stores and aeroplanes, but also on trains, a radio station, financial services, clothing, holidays, drinks and cosmetics. The brand is inextricably linked to Richard Branson and its personality shares many of his traits – both are charismatic, maverick and entrepreneurial. Virgin is dedicated to giving people what they want and has a reputation for challenging the conventions of the marketplaces it enters.

"The concept of 'bringing in' is going to turn the whole distribution system upside down."

boxes of groceries on bikes. And now people are saying, 'What a pity, we've got that wretched supermarket cart, and we'll be lucky if we find someone to load the shopping into the bags for us and then back into our cars. And then there's the awful social problem of all those nasty supermarkets and their car parks outside our town. What's happening to the centre of our town?' You could perhaps solve all of that by direct selling and home delivery. It's not the same as catalogue shopping, because we still want the touchy-feely bit. The ideal really for all of us is to have the pleasure of walking around Marks & Spencer or Harrods, but then not to have to cart the stuff home.

I THINK A LOT of popular brands today are really just fashion phenomena. The Body Shop is a good example of fashion retailing. It met a particular need at a time when people were fed up to the back teeth with certain kinds of retailing. Anita Roddick came along and said, 'Well, here it is, straightforward, pure stuff. None of it's been animal-tested. I'm offering you stuff in a plain bottle without any ballyhoo.' That was a unique brand positioning, but not for long. Other people come along and say 'Well, I can do that too, and better, or cheaper'. Propositions like that often falter because it's so difficult to find ways of constantly freshening the offering and beating back the newcomers.

IN TERMS OF brand prospects for the next 25 years, I think one could do far worse than to be involved in the leisure industry. It would be nice perhaps to own a cruise line of some sort, although they're quite thick on the ground or thick in the water these days. But look at the way in which the fortunes of P&O, for example, have been transformed since they stopped being a liner company and started providing floating holiday resorts. P&O now cover the entire spectrum of the marketplace, from the most luxurious to the most basic in cruising, in a way which is stunningly exciting and successful. That's an old brand, if you like, which has learned how to refresh itself.

ON A BROADER LEVEL, I think that one of the greatest challenges that we as human beings face over the next 25 years is the direction that our ethical values are going to take. We're emerging from a long period in which those values were provided to us by religion. Unfortunately, these days, the great majority of people have rejected that set of values, and I'm not sure what they've replaced them by. So it seems to me that the future is going to be heavily determined by the extent to which a positive set of replacement ethical values emerges either to replace religion or to bolster it up again. And the jury is very much out at the present time. Still, one has in the end a great deal of faith in the ability of mankind to find the right answers. Self preservation is not a bad driver..."

P&O

The Peninsular and Oriental Steam Navigation Company is better known to most of its customers simply as P&O. Since its foundation as a scheduled passenger liner service more than 160 years ago, P&O ships have flown the same red and yellow quartered flag, derived from the national colours of Portugal and Spain. Today, the most public images of this major international company are its white cruise ships and blue ferries, but it is also a worldwide port developer and has logistics and cold storage operations across Europe, in Australasia and the Americas, and substantial deep-sea container shipping interests.

"I think that a lot of people are just paying lip service to diversity."

Spike Lee set himself at the forefront of the Black New Wave in American cinema with his debut film, *She's Gotta Have It*, an independently produced comedy. Established as one of Hollywood's most influential film makers of the past decade, he has just completed his 11th film, *He Got Game*, starring Denzel Washington and Ray Allen. Outside the film industry, Spike has produced and directed numerous music videos and also works in the field of advertising commercials. His latest venture Spike/DDB is a full service advertising agency concentrating on the urban and ethnic minority markets.

"I KNOW THAT people can be brands, but I don't consider myself to be a brand; I think of myself as an artist. If I saw myself as a brand, that could create a conflict and could damage my integrity. But I think some people sometimes might see me as a brand; I guess it depends on who you're asking. To me, a brand is a name or a symbol that creates instant consumer recognition. Once they see that name they know exactly who the company is, they know the product, they know the standard that they provide. Some brands go one step further, they have a symbol, a non-verbal cue, which creates that instant consumer recognition. The Nike Swoosh is a great example of that.

FOR ME, Nike is the greatest brand in the world today. They are not where they were, but to me they still look the best. Phil Knight had vision; Nike wouldn't be here today otherwise. Someone starts out selling sneakers in the trunk of his car with the sole made by pouring foam into a waffle iron. People say you're crazy, but you prove them wrong. I've always been attracted to people who have vision, no matter what field they're in. Ted Turner, for instance, with CNN. You're going to have a TV station with news 24 hours a day? Put him in Bellevue. Eighth floor. But look who's laughing now.

SO, I WOULD have to say Nike is my favourite brand, and since I'm a big sports fan I would also have to say the New York Yankees. I travel all around the world and you see that interlocking N.Y. everywhere; people want to associate with the brand even if they've never even been to a match. Another interesting brand is Rolex. They have never had any TV ads, to my knowledge. They don't have to advertise, period. Now that is the best position to be in, where you don't have to advertise. You know you've really got it made then.

I GUESS MY relationship with the Nike brand has also been strengthened by my own work with the brand. I got a call from a guy at Weiden and Kennedy; he had seen my film *She's Gotta Have It* and wanted to put Mars Blackmon, the character I played in that film, together with Michael Jordan. It was shot in black and white and we went on to do those spots together for the next 7 or 8 years. I think Nike should be given great credit for having the vision and the courage to put their money behind an African-American. Even today, a lot of corporations are still hesitant about having an African-American representing them. There is a fear that somehow it would turn off the greater market. So, in that respect, Michael Jordan has definitely helped break the race barrier. Michael is a trend setter. He has done things on and off the court that no one else has done before. He's not just an athlete. An athlete has never been used to endorse products successfully the way Michael does, and by that I don't just mean Nike endorsement. Gatorade, MCI, Hanes, Ballpark Franks, we could go on and on. Michael really broke the mould.

IT WAS THE WORK with Michael that sparked my interest in advertising. As well as the Nike ads,

"I've always been attracted to people who have vision."

I did the campaign for Levi's button fly. That was fun. But then the more I did it, the less satisfied I became with just being the hired gun, being called in when everything was already planned and they just needed a director. And so I felt if I was given the opportunity, I would like to have an agency so that me and my team could get in at the ground floor and come up with the actual ideas in the first place. That's how this joint venture between myself and DDB got started. Our clients include Miami Heat, and we also have New Era, the manufacturer of all the baseball hats for major league baseball. Soft Sheen is another client, it's a black hair product company.

I WAS KEEN TO get involved in the agency, not just from a creative standpoint, but in order to make a statement to society and to start a process of change for the future. My thing is this. I think there is much more diversity in the film industry than the advertising industry, and there is hardly any diversity in the film industry! So, a lot of people are just paying lip service to diversity. Until people actually want to go out and actively seek it, the complexion in the industry is not going to change. And it's vital that this change happens in the future, if only to ensure that advertising is going to be as effective as possible. I just think that inherently there are some things that you might not know about, if you're trying to communicate with a section of the population who are different from you in a fundamental way. Just look at the demographics of this country and the world: it's over 50 per cent people of colour. So, it simply makes sense to me that if we want to reach consumers, our agencies should look like the consumers, at least to some extent. And obviously it's not just about what colour you are, but about your whole perspective on life. But if you go from agency to agency, it's really white, and the only way it's going to change is if people really decide this is a change they feel is valuable. If not, it's going to continue to be this way in the future. I often think that it's the agencies' fault, they should be more pro-active on this issue.

BUT OF COURSE I'm a novice in this industry, I'm not trying to speak like a sage. I'm not being humble when I say that, because I'm talking about Lee Clow and other giants. I come up short. They have done some great things, and have really helped to change the way we look at the world. Very rarely do you get a client who is willing to take a risk and try something different. Clients seem to want to do the same stuff again and again and again; people get too comfortable and they don't want to risk anything. They don't want to jeopardise the house in Greenwich; they're not going to put their neck on the line for some new work that may or may not be successful. So they are going to go for the same thing, that same pitch right down the middle of the plate and that just breeds mediocrity. That would be my message to clients of the future: take more risks!

IF I COULD sum up the next 25 years in one word, it would be *buy*. That is what I think, even now at this point in time in the history of the world; it's buy, buy, buy. We have a product and we want you to

Nike

Nike's credo 'Just do it' encapsulates the company's focus on innovation, athletics and leadership. Although the Nike name (the name of the Greek goddess of victory) was not adopted until 1971, the company began some years earlier, when the coach, Bill Bowerman, teamed up with the athlete, Phil Knight. Their ambition then, as now, was to help athletes perform better with innovative products such as the Waffle Trainer and the AirMax. Nike has also been largely responsible for turning the sports shoe into a fashion item. In recent years, Nike has been criticised for poor employment practice, which it is currently taking great pains to address.

"My fear for the future is that three companies own everything in the world."

buy it. And how are we going to do that? B-U-Y. Buy. My fear for the future is that 3 companies own everything in the world. You already see that starting now in the film industry with Universal buying Polygram. If 3 companies own everything in the world, it's not good. Certainly it's not good for artists. There will be fewer and fewer places where you can go. The fewer places you can go, the less good work is going to get made.

MEGA-COMPANIES HAVE so much power, and this power will only increase over the next 25 years, in my opinion. I've heard a lot about these companies trying to make positive changes in society, and I think it's really an individual choice as to whether companies want to do that or not. I think it depends on how much money they are making. The more money they make, the more willing they are to throw some crumbs into whatever charity or social issue they wish to support. I think everyone should do something, I think it's part of being a good corporate citizen. There's a great opportunity here for companies and brands to actively support diversity in ways other than their advertising, and obviously I think that's for the best.

WITH REGARD to other possibilities in the future, I don't have a crystal ball! So, you know, I can't tell what is going to happen in the future. Who knew that Russia would fall apart? The greatest brand in the next 25 years might not even be in existence now. It might emerge from technology that isn't even thought about yet. I think everybody would have to say it's going to be the Internet companies. That is the next frontier. In 25 years there might not even be stores anymore, you might just buy everything over the Internet. That would present an interesting advertising challenge!"

New Era

New Era Cap Co. was established by Ehrhardt Koch in 1920, in Buffalo, New York, as an all-American manufacturer of high quality caps. The company continues to meet the demands of today's athletes and sports fanatics and is the exclusive uniform cap of Major and Minor League baseball, as well as a licensee for the NBA, NFL, NHL and colleges across the US. With products which are competitively priced and of a high standard of quality, the New Era brand stands for 'going the extra mile' and is encapsulated in the corporate rallying cry 'Made from scratch and built to last by proud Americans'.

www.neweracap.com

"The brands that become creatively centred
will be the brands of the future."

Lee Clow is Chairman and Chief Creative Officer of TBWA Worldwide, renowned as one of the most innovative advertising agencies in the world. Responsible for many world famous advertising campaigns – Nike 'Air Jordan,' the 'Energizer Bunny' for Duracell and, most recently, 'Think Different' for Apple Computers – TBWA/Chiat/Day has, under his former direction, won some of the industry's highest accolades. To Lee, advertising isn't so much a business as an art form. Every campaign is an opportunity to express a company's point of view in the most engaging, imaginative and artistic way possible.

"BRANDS AREN'T just a way of remembering what you want to buy any more. They've become part of the fabric of our society. Brands are part of our system of ordering things – they even create context about who we are and how we live. Brands have become badges for people. They articulate who you are and what your values are. And brands aren't just articulated by their advertising any more; they're articulated by everything they do. Every aspect of a brand that touches people defines that brand. Today, with so much media, consumers have the ability to know more about a company than sometimes companies want them to know, and that's part of what brands have to deal with.

THINK ABOUT the whole Nike phenomenon. They did so many things that basically raised the bar and changed the rules in terms of what a brand could be and how it could create relationships with people. People bought Nike not because of what they made, but because of who they were. But at the same time, the media got a look in the back door and saw this stuff coming from the Far East. And that cast a negative pall over the brand, as well as the fact that it was becoming so ubiquitous that it lost its specialness. I think as brands get huge you hit these kinds of life stages. IBM had a life stage where you thought it was just going to disappear because it got so big and so monolithic. I have a lot of faith that Nike is going to figure out how to move to the next level, if they just work out how to manage their brand so that it doesn't rub people the wrong way.

IT'S A VERY INTERESTING thing; since the Russians gave up and there's no major terrifying war scenario, people are making big companies into villains these days. When you're small and feisty and have attitude and edge, when you're just doing it, you're cool. When you become so ubiquitous that you can put your logo on every jersey on every football team on the planet, all of a sudden people react and say 'I don't want anybody to be that big and that powerful.' That's the problem with Bill Gates and Microsoft – I don't think I like the richest man in the world. That's the weird dynamic that's going to have to be managed by successful brands.

BRANDS ARE part of capitalism. They're part of the free enterprise system. And I think if you grew up in America and if you've had some success in America you believe that's a pretty good system. Still, I think brands are going to have to start to contribute to society in order for people to want to do business with them. The Body Shop and Ben & Jerry's are good examples of brands that say, 'We're not just here to make money. We're here because we think there's something we can contribute to the world by doing our business the way we do it.' The reality today is that everything communicates. It's not just about media in the sense of buying an ad or getting a good PR company. So managing brands is going to be more and more about trying to manage everything that your company does. The smartest companies have already figured this out. Take Gap. They could just be a garment maker and instead they are a total concept. The environment of their stores is as important as their

"Managing brands is going to be more and more about trying to manage everything that your company does."

advertising which is as important as their catalogue which is as important as their website. Every new medium that has materialised has been managed in the context of the brand.

I THINK THAT the idea that the Internet is going to subsume all media relationships is totally bogus. If I'm shopping for a car and I don't want to visit a car dealer, I can go online and see the brochure; ultimately I might even be able to order my car. But I don't think that online is where I'm going to get the initial passion for that brand. Car showrooms may just become a place where I can touch and feel and smell the leather and I may do all my commerce someplace else. But I'm still going to need to get seduced by the brand before I want to go seek them out interactively.

ONE OF THE consequences of becoming a media society is that we have to think of people as an audience before we think of them as consumers. That's the crisis that the news media is having right now; people basically want you to package news with some entertainment, something more interesting than just the hard cold facts. I think that's why the Clinton thing kept going – it became entertainment for society. People felt, 'Well, as long as the economy is doing good, he's doing a good enough job for me and if the guy is a slut I can't do anything about it.' But they still tuned in every night instead of watching a soap opera. Now, when you introduce a new product you're almost putting on a show for people. You're saying 'Ta-daa!' And without the first 'Ta-daa!', people won't ask for any more information.

WHAT BRANDS do I think are classics? For me, Volkswagen Beetle is one. Who would have thought it? Here's this ugly little car designed by Adolf Hitler and yet it became so loved all over the world. They mismanaged the brand from a product standpoint for a number of years. But when they re-introduced the Beetle, immediately it recaptured all the spirit of the brand from the 60s and early 70s. They still had this latent relationship with people that they could tap into.

I REALLY BELIEVE that Apple is one of those enduring brands too. I have a very personal relationship with Apple because I was there when we introduced Macintosh and we kind of crafted the brand and tried to capture the soul of it. Steve Jobs was passionate about giving computers to people. It wasn't about becoming another business machine and it wasn't about how many boxes they could sell. It was really about saying if people could get their hands on this technology they could be better and they could be more creative and they could do things that they couldn't do before.

STEVE, WHEN he was 24 years old, said the computer is a bicycle for your mind. So he wasn't trying to make faster adding machines or better typewriters. He was trying to make a tool that could truly

Ben & Jerry's

Vermont initially experienced the irreverence of Ben Cohen and Jerry Greenfield when they opened their first ice cream parlour in a renovated filling station in 1978. Since then, Ben & Jerry's has become a leading brand of super premium ice cream, ice cream novelties, low fat ice cream, low fat yoghurt, sorbet, and Frozen Smoothies, using Vermont dairy products and high quality, all natural ingredients. Ben & Jerry's operates its business on a three-part mission statement emphasising product quality, economic return and a commitment to the community. Ben & Jerry's gives 7.5 per cent of its pre-tax profits back to the community through corporate philanthropy that is primarily employee led.

"One of the consequences of becoming a media society is that we have to think of people as an audience before we think of them as consumers."

better humankind and that was the thing that drove him to discover a very human interface. And when Steve left, the people that took over didn't understand that soul, that centre of the brand. They understood that Apple was a popular brand, a cool brand. But they just thought they could start trying to be all things to all people. When Steve came back he said, 'Okay, we're not going to be all things to all people. So let's just get back to what the soul of this brand is about.' It's putting technology in front of human beings to do something that they couldn't do before. It's not about running an office as much as empowering the individual. *Personal* computers. I think Apple believes in personal computers more than anybody but didn't have any new products to prove this. So the first thing we did was just try to celebrate our values and what we believed in – creativity, thinking outside the box, individual thinkers. And then somebody thought of Gandhi and we said 'Hey, why shouldn't we celebrate that whole insane notion that you can change the world? It's always been Apple's mantra. Why don't we celebrate the people who were crazy enough to think a whole different way about how things are done? Let's celebrate creative genius – let's celebrate the crazy ones.'

STEVE IMMEDIATELY eliminated something like 20 out of the 24 products that they made. Kept the 4 hardcore Power Macs that could do great desktop publishing. And had the designers get to work on making a new personal computer. Almost re-visiting the spirit of Macintosh. In less than a year Apple introduced iMac. And you know what? Thirty percent of iMac sales are to people that never had a computer before, moms and grandmas that can now e-mail their kids in college. So Apple is a brand that almost went out of business, but was able to dig down and connect with something in its soul that allowed it to live. I really believe that if it wasn't for what the Apple brand stood for, it couldn't have rebounded.

I THINK THE next century is going to have a ton to do with creativity. I think the thinkers, the idea people, the creative people on the planet are going to be the epicentre of what happens because it's not about manufacturing efficiencies and distribution. The brands that become creatively centred and idea centred will be the brands of the future. The dinosaurs will be the bureaucracies, the pass-it-down-the-line companies. It used to be: 'Let me have factories all over the planet with thousands of employees and I can rule the world.' Now it's going to be 'Give me the 10 most brilliant people in my industry and I can rule the world'. The companies that are going to succeed are those that harness the creativity of people".

Apple

Individualistic and anti-establishment, Apple started life in 1976, the brainchild of Steve Jobs and Steve Wozniak. Friendly, humorous and colourful, the logo epitomised Apple's difference from other players in the marketplace. The launch of the Macintosh in 1984, with its user-friendly icons, was a huge success; computers were no longer tools to be feared. Constantly innovating, Apple has recently launched the Apple Store, enabling customers to buy direct over the web and the telephone, and the award winning iMac, which makes the functional desirable. Apple has encouraged us all to 'Think different'.

"I think you have to build on the best of the past in order to create the future."

Sandra Dawson is the first woman to become Master of a former all-male college at Cambridge University. In 1995, she moved from Imperial College, London University, to become KPMG Professor of Management Studies, Director of the Judge Institute of Management Studies and a Fellow of Jesus College. Elected Master of Sidney Sussex College at the end of 1998, she took up her post in July 1999 and continues as Director of the Judge Institute. Sandra's specialisms are organisational behaviour, health management, innovation and technology transfer and she is the author of 3 books.

"SOMETIMES HERE in Cambridge, because of my subject and because I didn't come to Cambridge until I was 50, I'm looked on as a person who can talk about what the outside world is about. I think you have to build on the best of the past in order to create the future, and I think that Cambridge shows that it can change extremely well in anticipation of the future. Cambridge is a universally recognised international brand, and I think Oxford is the same, so are Harvard, Yale, Stanford and Princeton. In a way, I am proof of the way that Cambridge has changed: there aren't many business schools that have a woman as their director and I'm also Master Elect of Sidney Sussex, which is the first Cambridge college founded for men with a woman elected as its head.

HOWEVER, I'M NOT a great brand person, and I think my children thought it was very amusing that I should be asked for my thoughts on brands because they said, 'Mum, you don't know any!' and I said 'You'd be surprised!' My subject isn't marketing so I'm approaching this as the head of a business school and an ordinary punter. For me, brand is a name which implies a measure of quality, and over time, the name and the quality become synonymous. I'd look on a brand as a guarantee of quality, or a guarantee of a way of meeting my expectations in respect of a product or a service. Brands should be attracting people to them because they offer excellence.

I'M THINKING OF the household brands I grew up with. I remember going and buying butter in Sainsbury's, when they patted the butter up! You went to Sainsbury's for good value, high quality products which were readily available. That brand has been sustained and developed. Another brand is Hovis; to my generation, Hovis actually means good, nourishing brown bread. But there's a lot of good, nourishing brown bread around in all sorts of places now, so Hovis uses its heritage to distinguish itself from competitors who offer a similar product. But my personal favourite brand, although it certainly doesn't yet have worldwide appeal, is Long Tall Sally. I'm tall, so it's often very difficult to buy clothes. There's a small chain of four or five shops called Long Tall Sally and they consistently meet my expectations of quality. The company has established a specialism in a niche area, and in my view, that's going to be increasingly important for great brands of the future.

WITH REGARD TO great brands of today, I think of 'great' in terms of wide coverage; you can go anywhere and find them. Coca-Cola comes out very, very well – you can be in the middle of the African plain and you'll come across someone with a wheelbarrow containing three drinks, and one of them is likely to be Coca-Cola. It's a universal language. We get pictures from the other side of the world and see people everywhere wearing Nike or Reebok. There's bound to be a shrinkage of the world with regard to brands. I think it's quite interesting because some brands appear to be universal and yet they're differently interpreted in different places; you can go abroad and feel at home because there are these universal brands, but they'll have their own local interpretations. McDonald's

"Some brands appear to be universal, and yet they're differently interpreted in different places."

varies the ingredients of its burgers to accord with local religious and dietary sensitivities.

FOR ME, THE FUTURE is *glocalisation*. We're living in a global economy, but within that global economy, what's happening locally is going to be critical in determining what happens to business. The future is also going to be about *anticipation*, in both senses of the word. Anticipation, as in the excitement of what's possible, but also anticipation, as in predicting the enormous changes facing businesses. Businesses are getting better at anticipating; businesses that have been caught napping clearly see a reduction of market share or a predator finds them easy prey. I would say the brand is one major way to achieve business success and that you should always look at the brand as part of your business strategy. Essentially, I don't think you can develop a business strategy without looking at brands.

GREATER CONSIDERATION on the part of brand owners as to whether they are really living the values that they seek to portray in order to sell their brand would really benefit companies. If we look at the enormous increase in corporate power and realise that many large corporations have greater economic power than many countries, it does put an enormous responsibility upon those corporations to pay very strong regard to what they've got to do in this area. This means a greater acknowledgement in boardrooms that profitability can be secured at the same time as social and environmental sustainability. It's a realisation that important social and democratic values can be achieved without compromising efficiency and profitability along the way. So it's not a wishy-washy 'Why can't we all care more for each other?' It's building values into strong and realistic corporate governance. These are business decisions and so will be decided on business terms. Should brands become more ethically responsible? If we were addressing that question in the boardroom, then I would say, 'Think about the brand image that you're trying to portray. If that image has broader ethical considerations, what is the company doing about considering and acting on these issues?' Without an answer, I would be quite sceptical of the notion that a brand itself has meaningful values.

I'M OBVIOUSLY talking about this from a business point of view; I think it makes good business sense to be more ethically responsible. It's also morally 'good', but realistically, things that are just 'good' don't have a very strong track record of necessarily achieving change. So issues of sustainability have to be tied back to the business case. Some consumers already want to know what's going on behind the brands they buy, and perhaps more people will want to know in the future. But other people won't really be worried. Brands have such enormous symbolism – so long as some people are wearing the right label and they get the kudos they want, they won't care. So the important thing for the company is to know the nature of their market and their customers' motivations; there are very, very significant differences according to age, class, and background

University of Cambridge
The University of Cambridge is the second oldest university in the UK. It was founded early in the 13th century and counts among its alumni John Milton, Isaac Newton, John Harvard (later to endow Harvard University) and Charles Darwin. The university is made up of 29 undergraduate colleges and a number of other specialised colleges, among the best known of which are Trinity and King's, with its world-famous chapel. Cambridge's rivalry with Oxford is exemplified for many by the annual University Boat Race, dating from 1829. Cambridge has its own logo, its coat of arms, which was granted to the University in 1573 and is used on a wide range of applications including credit cards and sweatshirts.

UNIVERSITY OF CAMBRIDGE

"Realistically, things that are just 'good' don't have a very strong track record of achieving change. So issues of sustainability have to be tied back to the business case."

in terms of the way in which brands are subject to greater scrutiny.

LOOKING AHEAD, I think that whether we should be pessimistic or optimistic about the future depends a great deal on big business. I'm by nature an optimist, but I'll start with my worst-case scenario to get it out of the way. I think the worst-case scenario is that we have increasing inequality, that we have a very anomic, materialistic, individualistic society in which there's an increasing lack of social cohesion and in which caring for other people becomes less significant. And I think this will also cause enormous dislocations in society long-term. In a sense, you can say that all the developments of information technology, whilst they can facilitate greater social cohesion, can also cause dislocation. However, more optimistically, we can look forward to a society which values diversity, supports meritocracy and harnesses motivation to create a stronger economy and a better society. Advances in technology and the World Wide Web can, for example, be enormously beneficial for the delivery of education, as a means to increase access for people who have traditionally been outside formal education systems.

I THINK MORE brands will emerge on the Internet. Think about how brands used to emerge on billboards. You walked or you drove and there was a billboard. And even now, with television ads, it depends upon people actually coming into contact with your message. With the Internet, however, you can choose to metaphorically walk past a site anywhere in the world. The Internet allows you to do it yourself, to experience the product, talk about the service. You can do it in a more relaxed way; you're not subject to high pressure sales, because you, the customer, can take charge of the relationship, rather than being subordinate. What's going to happen to Amazon.com when e-commerce takes off? Will it do very well because it was first, or will other brands quickly follow and build a distinctive niche? I just bought a laptop computer through the Internet. It was *extraordinarily* easy! And for someone who doesn't particularly like spending their time going shopping, it was an *amazing* experience. So I'd look to the brands that are going to be created on the Web, and I think that they will take off much faster than we probably anticipate now.

FROM THE POINT of view of the Judge Institute within the University of Cambridge, we have got to make sure that we build our brand on the Web to a very high standard in comparison to our competitors. Already, we are finding an exponential increase in the number of student applications which come to us through the Web. I think that brands have to go to the people, take account of their motivations as well as create new desires, and I think that successful brands have already done that."

Amazon.com

Amazon.com, Inc. the Internet's No. 1 music, video and book retailer opened its virtual doors on the World Wide Web in July 1995. Today, the Amazon.com store has expanded to offer online auctions and more than 4.7 million book, music, video and game titles, plus secure credit card payment and streamlined ordering through 1-Click[sm] Technology. Amazon.com operates national websites: www.amazon.co.uk in the United Kingdom and www.amazon.de in Germany. Amazon.com also operates PlanetAll (www.planetall.com), a Web-based address book, calendar and reminder service, and the Internet Movie Database (www.imdb.com), an authoritative source of information on more than 150,000 movies and entertainment programmes.

"The best and most effective brands of the future will be built around knowledge."

Lord Puttnam CBE, Chairman of Enigma Productions, is David Puttnam, the Oscar-winning producer of *Chariots of Fire*, *The Killing Fields*, *Midnight Express* and *The Mission*. Chairman of Columbia Pictures from 1986 to 1988, he now works principally in the field of education, serving as an adviser to a number of government departments, as a governor and lecturer at the London School of Economics and as Chancellor of the University of Sunderland. He received a knighthood for his services to the British film industry in 1995 and was appointed to the House of Lords as a Life Peer in 1997.

"MY UNDERSTANDING of what a brand represents was formed by my early experiences in advertising. When I started my career in 1958, the components of advertising were really very simple, even unsophisticated – a product, a logo, a price, a stockist and a claim. The claim was invariably that the product was either 'new' or 'improved' or sometimes 'new and improved'. It was what you might describe as a 'customer ad', offering a product for sale which the public would probably at some point want; you might buy Dunlop instead of Avon, but one way or another you needed a new tyre.

THINGS HAD changed by the mid sixties. I guess it was around then that ads began to set out to convince human beings that their 'lifestyle' required certain products which they'd possibly never heard of, let alone thought about, and that, for the most part, they almost certainly didn't need. This was the beginning of what I'd now term 'consumer advertising', and it involved a completely different approach. There seemed to be a remarkable mood of confidence and optimism then, which I suppose made it possible. That same mood, in the mid 60s, allowed some quite extraordinary talents to develop in the advertising business.

THIS PARTICULAR type of consumer advertising has continued to evolve. Today a brand is almost always identified with a lifestyle choice, rather than with just a product. Virgin's an obvious example of a lifestyle brand; they have a range of products which extends from airlines to pensions and even bridal wear. I think most people would agree that the Virgin brand says something quite specific about the people who use its products; generally, that they're hip, young at heart and chic without being chi-chi.

ONE OF MY OWN favourite small brands is Papyrus, a London-based stationer. I have to confess to being something of a stationery fanatic. I suppose it's natural that stationery has tended to be very important to me – I've always generated a very considerable volume of correspondence – in fact, at one time I was writing over a hundred letters a week! It was my wife Patsy who first introduced me to Papyrus and since then I've become a devotee of their products. They are all beautifully crafted. Papyrus stationery seems to me quintessentially English, quite unlike anything else I've ever encountered in other parts of the world. I really do have something of a stationery obsession. I'm permanently looking for the world's perfect writing instrument. The closest thing I've found is yet another brand, but this time a much older one called Yard-O-Led – a pencil brand. I do have some favourite brands that aren't to do with stationery – for example, Connolly, who make the leather upholstery for Jaguar cars.

I'M NOT SURE I could tell you which brands will dominate our future; I rather suspect that some of

"Technology offers us a marvellous opportunity to create new brands which will contribute to our well-being as fully empowered citizens."

them have yet to be created. The industry I know best is the industry of moving images and digital technologies, so I'll give you an example from that. We're experiencing an ever increasing digital convergence between the printed word and television, computers and the Internet. This means that we're pretty rapidly seeing a blurring between many of the distinctions we've traditionally taken for granted; you can't really make a distinction between 'printed' and 'written' information any more. I understand that Internet traffic is doubling roughly every 100 days and, by 2002, it's predicted that electronic commerce could easily surpass £300 billion. So that's quite an exceptional rate of change.

I THINK IT'S clear that this new online world is going to be driven by 'virtual' brands every bit as much as the more tangible world of physical goods and services. You're already seeing some of the astonishing effects of this convergence. Yahoo! was only launched in 1994, but, by some accounts, it's now worth more than General Motors, Texaco and Merrill Lynch. Amazon.com, the online bookseller, was recently quoted as having a value of $25 billion – despite the fact that it's yet to turn a dollar of profit. Those are both stunning examples of brands that have sprung up virtually overnight. All their reputation has been built on speed and quality of service. But they're a completely new and different kind of service brand; there's no traditional face-to-face contact, just technological interaction. And the Internet isn't just creating technological brands like Yahoo!. Electronic commerce is having an effect on every area of our lives, and it's spreading rapidly. Physical interaction, going into shops, is hardly necessary at all. Think of any type of product and service – buying the weekly groceries, investing in stocks and shares – and today you can probably trade it on the Internet. And if you can't now, you'll soon be able to.

SO I'D EXPECT to see a great proliferation of this type of 'virtual brand' – brands which aren't so much goods in themselves, but provide the means to access goods and, perhaps even more importantly, to access information. Peter Drucker said something very powerful in his book *Post Capitalist Society*. 'Knowledge is the only meaningful resource today'. In the 21st century, I expect that the world's greatest brands will be even more closely linked to access to high quality and reliable knowledge and information. I suspect for instance that we'll have branded products which provide the equivalent of a daily digital 'read out' – giving us all the information we need to monitor the effects of our diet, our exercise needs and the overall state of our health.

THE RATE OF technological change is breathtaking; its implications are so far-reaching and its consequences so unpredictable that the future is in every respect there for the making – and the taking. I think it's inevitable that some of today's technology brands will suffer – maybe even an apparently unassailable brand like Microsoft. Think of what happened to IBM a few years back – there's a clear precedent for apparently ground-breaking technology-based brands getting overtaken

Papyrus

Over the years Papyrus has become the first choice for people in the UK looking for high quality stationery and desk and writing accessories with style. Papyrus is totally committed to good design: they print and diestamp the very best writing paper and social stationery and produce an exclusive range of leather and marbled desk accessories, occasional books and albums, using traditional English craftsmen. Customers visiting their 2 shops in London and Bath find helpful and well-informed staff and their mail order catalogues reach a worldwide clientele. A website is being developed to increase Papyrus' brand presence in the export market.

PAPYRUS
·PRINTERS & STATIONERS·

"If we continue down the path we appear to have chosen, the danger exists that we will end up exactly where we appear to be heading."

by the competition. I see technology as offering us a marvellous opportunity to create some new brands which can make a vital contribution to our wellbeing. They'll help us become fully empowered citizens with a real sense of opportunity, not just passive consumers. But if we just resort to 'giving the people what they want' then I fear we could very quickly run into trouble. The best and most effective brands of the future will be built around knowledge.

IF I LOOK AHEAD to the development of society over the next 25 years, I have a number of very real concerns. It's some years now since American Vice-President Al Gore's pessimistic warning of a society divided between information 'haves' and 'have nots', but his warning remains just as valid, just as pertinent today – in fact, perhaps even more so. In my view, we've got to ensure that the gap between the haves and the have nots doesn't simply mirror existing economic and social inequalities. In particular, we have to ensure that we don't accidentally create an information under-class of 'info-peasants', who, simply because of lack of access to learning in general and to new technologies in particular, find themselves permanently excluded from the shiny new Information Age of the 21st century. I believe that the answer, unsurprisingly, lies in education; it's only by creating a genuine educational opportunity for everyone that we can hope to lay the foundations of a truly inclusive community.

IN THE LEARNING society of the 21st century it will become ever more important to develop creative and imaginative brands which people can really trust and which deliver real benefits to our educational system. This is especially true since educational software will increasingly replace traditional 'chalk and talk' teaching methods.

TO QUOTE A Chinese proverb 'If we continue down the path we appear to have chosen, the danger exists that we will end up exactly where we appear to be heading.' I think those innovators who create the enduring brands of the 21st century can probably do as much as anyone to ensure that we avoid that fate."

Yahoo!

Yahoo! was created in 1994 as a guide to the favourite websites of two Ph.D students at Stanford University. Today Yahoo! Inc. is a global Internet media company that offers a branded network of comprehensive information, communication and shopping services to 60 million users worldwide. As the first online navigational guide to the Web, Yahoo! is the leading guide in terms of traffic, advertising, household and business user reach, and is one of the most recognised brands associated with the Internet. The company's global Web network includes 18 world properties.

YAHOO!

"I think it would be tragic if the creative engine for the world was simply Western European and American pop culture."

Graham Mackay is Group Managing Director of South African Breweries, the world's 4th largest brewing group, with operations in South Africa, Eastern Europe and China. Brought up in Swaziland, Natal and Rhodesia, Graham worked for BTR prior to joining South African Breweries in 1978. Initially responsible for Information Systems in the beer division, he rose to the position of Chairman in 1992. In 1994 he was appointed CEO of SAB Group and became Group Managing Director in 1997. Other directorships include Standard Bank of South Africa and Southern Sun Hotel Holdings.

"WE DON'T SELL beer anywhere, we sell brands. The difference revolves around what consumers are prepared to pay for, what they think makes something relevant to them, what aspirational connotations they add into their selection criteria; they're not just buying on price. To what extent have they started to broaden their range of aspirations beyond their domestic village? If they haven't, there is no role for brands. Then it's just a tacit contract between the consumer and the little brewery around the corner; he knows it produces stuff he likes, and his father drank the stuff before him, and so on. What he doesn't have is an ability to raise himself above that and choose between competing offerings. He can't choose between his village brewery and the brewery in the next valley or for that matter in the next country. Branding is vital in that progression.

BRAND CHOICE IS usually a lot more important in the Third World than in the First World; even though the consumer's expenditure is much lower, the investment he makes in each choice is much higher. The consequence of error to him is much greater, so he really needs to trust the brand. He does a lot of research with his peer group, checks opinions by discussion, invests time and attention. Even in South Africa, which is relatively sophisticated among the markets we operate in, the amount of emotional energy that goes into choosing a beer brand is far, far higher than it is in the West. Maybe in the West the outlay in dollar terms is far higher and the margin that you can beg of a premium brand is much higher. The point is that from the individual's perspective, the brand choices are much more important here than they are over there. It is also a lot more difficult to manipulate the consumer overtly because he often doesn't have access to media or the media doesn't have much access to him.

MY OWN INTEREST in brands is really commercial. I think that a brand should be measured by its ability to contribute a margin above its cost of production or above its peers. A brand's worth is rooted in its ability to deliver a reliable, expanding, long-lasting stream of commercial value to its owners. If it doesn't deliver that, then it might perhaps create a reputation, a mental furniture of some kind, but it wouldn't be a useful brand in my opinion. A reputation is not a brand, a heritage is not a brand, a collection of mental attributes and associations by themselves are not a brand, however interesting they may be. A brand must have the ability to deliver an interesting margin stream.

I THINK ONE of the greatest brands in the world is certainly Coca-Cola. It's got to be in the top 2 or 3 by anyone's reckoning. There are some other brands that I think have done a fantastic job – Mercedes-Benz, Rolls-Royce years ago (although they've lost their way), Benetton, Levi's, Harley-Davidson. Harley-Davidson's a most extraordinary brand considering the lack of technology in the product; in fact the brand's almost pure image. There's a very interesting thing about brands like Harley – I've always had a sneaky feeling that it's a brand that created itself as much as was created

"I think that issues like the preservation of natural resources and the environment will start to be important to brand consumers."

Jorge Cárdenas, General Manager of the National Federation of Coffee Growers of Colombia, is recognised as a world authority on coffee issues. A law graduate with a management Masters from Syracuse, New York, he joined the Colombian Coffee Federation in 1963. Besides managing Colombia's most important export product, Jorge is a member of the National Council of Economic and Social Policy. He is also President of the Colombian Entrepreneurial Group for the Economic Relationship with Japan, President of the Colombian Delegation to the International Coffee Board and special counsellor on coffee issues for the United Nations and Great Britain.

"BRANDS HAVE BECOME fundamental assets for businesses today; everyone tries to market their products under a brand name. Through brands, corporations acquire prestige and become accepted by the public. Anybody can make a product and distribute it, but it is very important for a brand to occupy a well-defined space within the market. In the last few decades, generic or 'white' brands were established for marketing purposes, but they were not successful with consumers. More recently, private labels entered the scene and were more successful because of the backing provided by the company name. Well-established brands are fundamental to the success of major corporations. Consequently, companies today are strongly focused on the way they manage their brands. Additionally, consumers start to associate brands with a certain level of quality and service; this guarantee of consistency is very important in today's industrial and commercial worlds. Of course, brand development represents a significant investment for corporations, and companies therefore need to achieve a price premium, as well as consumer loyalty, for their branded products.

AT A GLOBAL LEVEL, clearly Coca-Cola stands out as a very important global brand. Ford is also a great name. Quaker is another well-positioned brand; the Quaker name and identity have been associated with cereal products for a long time and the brand is very well recognised within its sector. Here in Latin America, the number of brands with powerful corporate backing is increasing, particularly in sectors like foods and beverages. I can think of several brands with a long tradition and a high level of international consumer recognition, for example Bimbo, Colcafé, Corona and Concha y Toro.

WITHIN COLOMBIA TODAY, there are a number of important national brands like Bavaria, Noel, Colombina and Luker. And, interestingly, brands such as Colombina and Noel are now exported. But the product that is at the forefront of most people's minds when they think of Colombia is coffee. Without a doubt, we have succeeded in creating a brand in this sector. Our brand development process has included education of farmers, quality control and careful product preparation, selection and promotion. And because of our branding work (and our significant promotional efforts), Colombian coffee, which is really just a commodity, has been able to set itself apart from other types of coffee, with its own niche within the high quality coffee market. It has succeeded because of its consistently high quality; when your product is reliable and doesn't change from day to day, you quickly find consumer acceptance and demand. It has been particularly important for us to concentrate on issues of quality. The Colombian Coffee Federation has therefore ensured that every step of the coffee growing process is quality controlled, starting from the first moment that the crop is planted. We carry out extensive training programmes with coffee growers, where we tell them the results of our technical research. We are active at every step of the production chain, because we need to make sure that 'Café de Colombia' will continue to support a premium price.

"In terms of new brands, I think that Asia and Eastern Europe will both be good seedbeds."

THE JUAN VALDÉZ NAME and figure were created for the Colombian Coffee Federation 40 years ago by DDB Needham in New York. The intention was to create a symbol to represent the Colombian coffee grower, to represent his way of life. The name was chosen after a good deal of research, because it was easy to pronounce in different languages. During the 40 years of the Colombian coffee campaign, our work has been very focused. First of all, we needed to identify Colombia as a coffee producing country. Then we progressed to show the environment in which Colombian coffee grows, the care we take of our natural resources, and later we began to educate people about the types of plantations and families involved. All this served to highlight that coffee growing is intensive family work; it involves skilled craftsmen and everyone has to play their part in order to produce a top quality crop.

THE JUAN VALDÉZ FIGURE was launched with a message: here we have the work of a craftsman, a product that is produced with great care, that enjoys an environment with lots of sun and good soil, and that is chosen bean by bean. Over the 40 years of the Juan Valdéz campaign, our message has evolved and become more sophisticated. For example, we began to show the product in different surroundings and identified it as a beverage which is suitable for everyone and for all occasions, a pleasant and healthy natural drink. More recently, we have gradually started to think about how to deliver the message of Colombian coffee to the consumer segments with the highest potentials for coffee consumption.

THE JUAN VALDÉZ BRAND is unique in that there is no other brand of raw coffee – although of course there are lots of important consumer coffee brands. Twenty years ago, when the coffee producing countries thought about launching a generic campaign to stimulate coffee consumption, they explored a number of options for developing an appropriate brand. Some of the people working on the project suggested the Juan Valdéz brand. The idea was that Colombia would share its brand with other countries, instead of having it as an exclusive asset. The consultants who were looking at the issue thought that this would be a better idea than creating a new name, since the Juan Valdéz brand was already recognised. There was talk of paying the Colombian Coffee Federation somewhere between 9 and 10 million dollars for the brand; today we would expect a much bigger figure! After all, we estimate that Colombia has invested more than a billion dollars in the Juan Valdéz brand in the 40 years since its creation. Despite labour intensive practices which increase the costs of coffee production in Colombia compared with other countries, Colombian coffee is able to command higher prices than other coffees which do not enjoy the same care and quality control; I believe that our brand helps us do this.

COMPETITION, efficiency and quality are words I would use to define the world's immediate future.

Corona

Corona Extra, the flagship beer for Grupo Modelo, has been the top-selling beer in Mexico for many years, and today reigns as Mexico's leading export. It is the number one imported beer in the United States, and every day millions of people in over 140 countries around the world are encouraged to 'change their whole lattitude' (sic). Founding its first brewery in 1925, Grupo Modelo is proud of its heritage and still brews all its beer brands in Mexico. Corona is an active sponsor of sporting events such as boxing and Indycar racing, and has a 14 year old relationship with the singer Jimmy Buffett.

"Many highly respected brands will become secondary trademarks beneath another great brand."

Society is becoming better educated and more culturally aware; as a result, people are becoming more demanding in their product choices. Technological and scientific development will improve communication, education and training, which will make ordinary people much more capable. Commerce and industry will have to become increasingly responsive in terms of quality, efficiency and timely client service. Brands will have to inspire confidence in consumers, who will become increasingly brand literate. In addition, I think that issues like the preservation of natural resources and the environment will start to be important to brand consumers. It will also be important to have ethical and professional values in business. Brands that try to manipulate consumers or break trading rules will be punished. As a result, increased competition, consumer pressure and regulatory pressure will force companies to have high ethical standards.

THE BRANDING LANDSCAPE will definitely change over the next 25 years. In terms of new brands, I think that Asia and Eastern Europe will both be good seedbeds. The process of merger and acquisition is so dynamic that it is hard to tell what will happen to many great brands of today; many may disappear, even though this may seem highly improbable now. In the automobile industry, for example, I believe many highly respected brands will become merely secondary trademarks beneath another great brand. With regard to coffee, I think that brands like Nescafé, Maxwell, Folger, Tchibo and Lavazza will continue to play an important role in the industry; so much investment already supports these brands. In the future, I believe that these brands will not only be used on the products we already know, but also on new products and new services which will meet new consumer needs. So, for example, I foresee the introduction of ready-to-drink beverages under these great brand names.

LOOKING AHEAD more generally, I see a bright future for our home-grown brands, provided regional trade integration and investment facilitate the process. Cheaper and easier access to multinational commercial TV will continue to support the growth of Western brands such as Coca-Cola, Ford, VW, General Electric and IBM. As in the case of our regional brands, this implies higher levels of free trade and foreign investment, so that branded products can be available in any national market. In conclusion, a brand will continue to be useful in the future only if it offers consistency and personal satisfaction to the consumer, over and above price. Ultimately, a brand stands for consumer loyalty, and this loyalty should translate into sales. Investing in a brand that does not generate consumer loyalty is a waste of money."

Nescafé

Nescafé made its first appearance in 1938 and has since become synonymous around the world with quality instant coffee. After over 60 years of innovative development, including most recently a new, sophisticated jar and an improved aroma, Nescafé is now the world's leading coffee brand and is a household name in over 100 countries. The brand has continued to keep pace with changes in consumers' tastes and has introduced a number of successful sub-brands such as Nescafé Cappuccino and Nescafé Frappé to cater for local needs. The brand seeks to place itself at the heart of social interaction, and its recent 'Open Up' campaign emphasises this.

"Since people will have less time, they're going to be seeking experiences which bring them some kind of instant self-actualisation."

Jo Harlow is Reebok's Vice President of Western Europe, with responsibility for Reebok France and operations in Italy and Switzerland. After graduating from Duke University with a BSc in Psychology, Jo joined Procter & Gamble. She then moved to Reebok in 1992 as footwear manager in the Southern California region and progressed to hold other positions including General Manager and regional Vice President, until her promotion to Vice President US Brand Marketing in 1996. Prior to her current position, she was Vice President of Marketing for Europe.

"THE REAL challenge for brands in the future will be to use the force of their personality to cut through all the information that's bombarding consumers. The sheer amount of information that consumers are exposed to today means that people don't have enough time even to synthesise everything they see, never mind getting a feeling for the brands they encounter. So only the clearest, most differentiated and most consistent brands will be able to break through. This means that brands need to be what I call 'choiceful'; they need to decide where and how to appear, based on their personality. Too many brands are just plastering their names on the jerseys of soccer players. I think that the definition of what a brand is has definitely changed over the years. Brands years ago just used to be about the features and benefits of an individual product under a trade name. Today, I think brands are infused with much more meaning.

IF A CONSUMER buys Reebok versus Nike, they're buying into the way that Reebok operates, our commitment to human rights. They know we care about how and where and under what conditions our products are made, versus what they have heard about Nike or other competitors. So they're buying into the total proposition, not just product features and benefits. If a consumer buys a pair of Nike versus Adidas, they're not just buying into the fact that the cushioning is better. They're buying into the attitude of Nike – the emotion, the athleticism and the aspiration of being a professional athlete that Nike has portrayed.

THIS IS GOING TO become more and more important over the next 25 years. There are a couple of reasons for this. First of all, the amount of information that's available to us now compared to 25 years ago is extraordinary – and it's increasing all the time. Consumers today find it much easier to compare individual products and to hear the views of other consumers. As a result, the intangible features of the brand become even more important in decision-making.

THE SECOND REASON IS a growing social instability. Certainly, at least from an American point of view, your job used to define you. At the same time as employment has become less secure, the role of the family and of religion has declined. Taken together, this has created a void in society. To some extent, therefore, brands have taken on the role of defining who people are, as opposed to simply being something that they wear or drink. I'm not just talking in materialistic terms, although clearly a Rolex watch gives a message about the wealth of an individual. I think that, as the personalities of brands become more defined and differentiated, individuals take on that personality. You'd 'give' a different personality to a 15 or 16 year old who wears one of the surf brands, like AirWalk, versus one who wears a more traditional brand like Nike or Reebok.

I THINK THESE brand choices are fairly conscious for most people. Consumers look for signals of

"I think that one of the top challenges of consumer marketing in the 21st century will be the proliferation of information."

Gary Lyon is an independent consultant specialising in the consumer healthcare sector. A graduate from the Ivey Business School, Canada, Gary has a 20-year track record working with pharmaceutical companies in Canada, the USA, Hong Kong and the UK. His career began with Procter & Gamble; he then moved to Schering Plough before joining Merck & Co where he rose to the position of General Manager responsible for the Canadian OTC business. In 1996 he joined Glaxo Wellcome as General Manager for Global OTC operations prior to completing his MBA/DIC at Imperial College.

"WHAT DO I think is the most powerful brand in the world today? I guess I'd have to say the Roman Catholic Church. It fulfils most of the criteria of a great brand: it's got superb visibility, high awareness and it's pretty consistent across its different manifestations. It's also growing in many parts of the world. But, like many brands, it's facing challenges – fragmentation, competition, how to respond to changing consumer needs. Despite this, I'd still say that it's one of the most important brands on the planet.

MY PERSONAL favourite brand is rather different – Starbucks. I'm a coffee drinker, so I have an affinity with the product to start with, but what I really admire about them is their great attention to detail. There's terrific continuity across their product line, rather like McDonald's. Starbucks is a great success story. The Starbucks team kept on going through the growth phase that kills most entrepreneurial endeavours and managed to keep the quality right even when they could no longer control every detail personally. Starbucks is also aggressive and expansionistic. They're my tip for the future.

MY PARTICULAR AREA of expertise is the pharmaceutical industry. Branding is relatively new there. In the past, pharmaceutical products have been very much locally driven, primarily because of differing regulations, so most marketing activity has been targeted at local audiences, like doctors, governments and health insurance schemes.

THREE EXCITING THINGS are happening now which should pave the way for the emergence of strong pharmaceutical brands. The first of these is European convergence. The development of the European Union has simplified the drug registration procedure and has led to infrastructure convergence, so there's a lot more similarity in terms of pricing, distribution and so forth. The second change is the emergence of lifestyle drugs, drugs which do not solve life-threatening illnesses, but correct dysfunctions or enhance quality of life. Traditional payers, authorities like the NHS and insurance companies, have not been terribly enthusiastic about funding such products; they think that the patient ought to pay more of the burden for this kind of drug. That means that pharmaceutical companies now have to consider how to talk directly to patients, rather than speaking to them via intermediaries. And then the third, probably most critical, factor is that consumers themselves have changed. We're all much more demanding, much better informed, much less willing to accept the first piece of advice we get from anyone or the first thing we read about a brand. We're much more into questioning, challenging, taking stock of our situation. The Internet is one dramatic example of this but it's by no means the only one. You look at the proliferation of specialist magazine titles in your newsagent; look at television, where the advent of cable has made room for niche programmes. Altogether these 3 factors have combined to create a climate which is ripe for brand development.

"There's an important lesson in branding. It can't be done quickly. It's not cheap. It takes long-term commitment and vision."

OF COURSE, THERE are some well-known pharmaceutical brands out there today. Zantac was one of the earliest blockbusters and certainly one of the most popular drugs of all time, in terms of the number of prescriptions written. Prozac and Viagra are 2 others that spring to mind. But as brands I think they're all lacking in some respects. Patients may be aware of them, but I don't think you'd find a lot of emotion attached to the brand names, like you would with Coca-Cola. You might know that Zantac is something to do with ulcers, but would you be able to say what its core essence or proposition is? The strongest brands are those that elicit an emotional response. Take the car industry. BMW and Mercedes both deliver very strong rational benefits in terms of precision engineering and drive ability, but they also speak of prestige, the best in their class. And in the long term those emotional benefits are as important as the rational ones.

IN THE PHARMACEUTICAL INDUSTRY, you see more of these emotional benefits in the OTC (over the counter) sector, where companies typically can talk directly to consumers. In fact the real opportunity for brand building lies in the switch of *prescription only* medicines to *over the counter* status. There's a tremendous opportunity for companies to create a strong, emotional, branded proposition at the prescription stage, so that the transition to OTC is less dramatic. In the past, particularly when switching a product, if you didn't get a quick return, support would tend to melt away. But you really need to stick at it, which isn't something pharmaceutical companies have been very good at. The Advil-Nuprin story is a good illustration of the tenacity you need to succeed as a strong brand-owner. In the mid 1980s ibuprofen went OTC in the US and 2 brands were launched at about the same time: Advil from American Home Products and Nuprin from Bristol Myers Squibb. For the first couple of years it was pretty much a dogfight. There were some small differences between the products in terms of pill size and colour and that kind of stuff, but American Home Products simply made it work. They took the long-term view and poured a tremendous amount of money into the brand. They just outslugged their competitor. Nuprin today is a nonentity in the US market. It's a great product, as good as Advil from an efficacy perspective, but it didn't receive the same level of sustained investment. In the US now Advil is known as advanced medicine for pain and its differentiated positioning has made it one of the leading analgesic brands. Therein lies an important lesson in branding. It can't be done quickly. It's not cheap. It takes long-term commitment and vision, and the companies that are prepared to do this will be the ones who ultimately win.

THE NEXT 25 years are going to be very exciting in the pharmaceutical industry. It's practically a wide-open book. There'll definitely be a major shakeout in terms of players and we'll see much more industry consolidation. There's also going to be a lot more direct-to-consumer activity – television advertising, Internet sites and so on. Still, I don't know if we'll see any pharmaceutical brands amongst the world's greatest brands in 25 years' time. Brands have to drive customer delight, to find ways and means of exceeding customers' expectations, rather than just meeting them.

Prozac

Since its launch in 1988, Eli Lilly's wonder drug Prozac has been prescribed for more than 17 million people in the US alone. Prozac was the first of a new class of antidepressants known as selective serotonin reuptake inhibitors (SSRIs). It has been suggested that Prozac marks the advent of a new pharmaceutical trend towards the development of 'lifestyle' drugs which enhance quality of life, rather than solve life-threatening disease. Like many great brands, Prozac has become part of the fabric of society, as is witnessed by books like *Prozac Nation*, a best seller written by Elizabeth Wurtzel.

In patients with depression…
PROZAC®
fluoxetine hydrochloride

"I think that the great brands of the future will not be corporate or product brands, they'll be service brands."

HOWEVER, I don't believe it's impossible to delight customers in healthcare. Brand delivery will be about not only solving healthcare problems, but about providing aftercare and services as well. Part of the challenge is going to be finding more innovative ways to target potential users. For example, we don't just want people to remember that they used Zovirax last time they had a cold sore and that it worked; we want to remind them to buy Zovirax before they have the next cold sore – maybe mailing them in the winter, or sending them some money-off coupons for a scarf to prevent the cold sore developing. There is a danger that we'll run into consumer fatigue. I think that one of the top challenges of consumer marketing in the 21st century will be the proliferation of information. Consumer targeting's got to be seen to be helpful and not intrusive, and I can't say that there's any magic formula there. The better I understand you, your needs, your habits, the more I can connect you with my brand.

I THINK THAT the great brands in the future will not be corporate or product brands, they'll be service brands. At the moment you have personal trainers who talk to you about your health, your lifestyle and your goals, and then devise a specific exercise programme for you. Well, I think in the future, there will be personal information managers, people who come to your home, do a very detailed interview about your lifestyle and interests and then go away and make it happen. They will screen your gazillions of emails, direct mail, phone calls, as well as new media stuff that hasn't even been invented yet, to ensure that you don't get information overload.

IN THE PHARMACEUTICAL sector, I can imagine the emergence of an important service brand, over and above a corporate or product brand. It could be called something like Health.com, and would handle you from cradle to grave, responding to your changing health and lifestyle circumstances. It could give you feedback on weekly blood test results that you do at home, advise you on your diet, what air filters you should have for where you're living and where you're working. If you move, it could tell you how you need to adapt your exercise regime and diet to compensate for the local environmental factors. It could also give you information about any drugs you might have to take and how to maximise their benefits. Of course, it would all have to be wrapped up with some kind of virtual product placement to make it commercially viable. I definitely think it's going to be an exciting few years."

Viagra

Viagra was introduced by Pfizer in 1998 as the first licensed oral treatment for erectile dysfunction (impotence). This distressing condition affects up to 1 in 10 men – and their partners. Viagra was developed to provide an effective, convenient treatment that would allow the condition to be managed by family doctors rather than hospital specialists only. The Viagra name and distinctive blue diamond format have become part of the vernacular and have bolstered Pfizer's reputation as the world's most innovative pharmaceutical company. It has also helped change the lives of thousands of men and women, by reducing the taboos surrounding the condition.

"Magic is important in people's lives,
so leaders must cater for that need for
the magical, the miraculous."

Deepak Chopra, MD, is Chairman and Co-Founder of the Chopra Center for Wellbeing in California. Formerly Chief of Staff at New England Memorial Hospital, he also taught at Tufts University and Boston University Schools of Medicine. Recognised for his role in bringing traditional Eastern principles to the Western world, he is the best selling author of over 20 books and more than 30 audio, video and CD Rom programmes, published in every continent and in dozens of languages. Dr Chopra teaches mind body techniques and education programmes worldwide.

"YOU KNOW what happened with this interview? I almost sensed the first question: 'What does the word 'brand' mean to you?' My personal definition of a great brand would be a name that immediately evokes a sense of leadership in any field. That's what I'd like it to be, anyway. The answer came to me intuitively, and a little while later what I did was, I took out a piece of paper and said to myself 'What does 'leadership' really mean to me in a brand? What might it mean for the future of a brand?' And I wrote down a few things; what I wrote down happened to be an acronym of the word LEADERS.

BRAND LEADERS, in fact all leaders, have the following qualities. L stands for 'Looking into the future', having a vision and having the ability to communicate that vision to the world with passion and trustworthiness. E stands for 'Empowerment', having the ability to convey a sense that we, the company behind the brand, are very powerful and we can empower you as well. That involves the ability to enrol the world at large in every activity, the promotion of well-being, whatever it is. It's the ability to give people a sense of being powerful: we can enrol you in our dream. Come with us so we can all benefit! This involves a great deal of sensitivity about the dreams of other people. It also involves feedback, communicating and being responsive to feedback. So, that's E. A is 'Awareness', which simply means asking yourself the question, 'Who am I? Who are we? What do we want?' And the next question, 'What is our purpose?' And of course for our audiences, 'Who are they? What do they want? What's their purpose?' So, it's an awareness of the many levels in society. It comes from a sense of a universal being. It comes from a brand's ego. There's a realm of our awareness, where we're focusing purely on personal things, asking ourselves how we can help, how we can serve. Where do I fit in the big puzzle?

D IS 'DOING'. It's not just about making these fancy statements, it's about being action-oriented. It's about the ability to take risks through your actions. It's about making very specific targeted plans. It's about acting as a role model, not through words only. Again, it's about being responsive to feedback, which means, am I doing what I say I will do or what I say I'm doing? E is 'Entering into a world of creativity', and brand leaders are those willing to relinquish their past and embrace ambiguity and uncertainty. They are willing to adapt to and learn from their mistakes. The creative brands have the ability to reach people through a very refined sense of sensory awareness. I've noticed that one of the things that makes a brand familiar to us is the visual symbol that represents it. Nike has a symbol. Coca-Cola has a symbol. A few brands have sound symbols as well; if I heard the United jingle in the bathroom in Tokyo, I would immediately think of United Airlines, a friendly sight! There are a few brands that even have smell symbols, but most of them are just perfume brands. I can see a company with lots of creativity actually moving from this position to a higher level of refined sensory awareness, where they can convey their message at a very high level of sensitivity.

The world's most valuable brands league table 1999

	Brand name	Country of origin	Brand value $US m	Market capitalisation of parent company $US m	Branded revenue 1998 $US m	Brand value as a multiple of branded revenue 1998	Brand strength score
1	Coca-Cola	US	83,845	142,164	16,932	4.95	82
2	Microsoft	US	56,654	271,854	14,484	3.91	80
3	IBM	US	43,781	158,384	81,667	0.54	75
4	General Electric	US	33,502	327,996	95,314	0.35	71
5	Ford	US	33,197	57,387	110,723	0.30	72
6	Disney	US	32,275	52,552	18,800	1.72	79
7	Intel	US	30,021	144,060	26,273	1.14	74
8	McDonald's	US	26,231	40,862	12,421	2.11	78
9	AT&T	US	24,181	102,480	53,223	0.45	70
10	Marlboro	US	21,048	112,437	9,743	2.16	74
11	Nokia	Finland	20,694	46,926	15,542	1.33	64
12	Mercedes	Germany	17,781	48,326	64,053	0.28	78
13	Nescafé	Switzerland	17,595	77,490	7,954	2.21	79
14	Hewlett-Packard	US	17,132	54,902	47,061	0.36	65
15	Gillette	US	15,894	42,951	4,147	3.83	80
16	Kodak	US	14,830	24,754	13,406	1.11	71
17	Ericsson	Sweden	14,766	45,739	22,741	0.65	63
18	Sony	Japan	14,231	28,933	57,143	0.25	75
19	Amex	US	12,550	35,459	19,132	0.66	71
20	Toyota	Japan	12,310	85,911	101,543	0.12	68
21	Heinz	US	11,806	18,555	7,367	1.60	75
22	BMW	Germany	11,281	14,662	25,935	0.43	74
23	Xerox	US	11,225	27,816	19,846	0.57	68
24	Honda	Japan	11,101	30,050	52,403	0.21	64
25	Citibank	US	9,147	42,030	23,525	0.39	67
26	Dell	US	9,043	97,327	18,243	0.50	57
27	Budweiser	US	8,510	26,036	6,106	1.39	69
28	Nike	US	8,155	10,565	8,951	0.91	71
29	Gap	US	7,909	20,481	5,433	1.46	60
30	Kelloggs	US	7,052	13,445	6,762	1.04	70

	Brand name	Country of origin	Brand value $US m	Market capitalisation of parent company $US m	Branded revenue 1998 $US m	Brand value as a multiple of branded revenue 1998	Brand strength score
31	Volkswagen	Germany	6,603	22,071	33,800	0.20	73
32	Pepsi-Cola	US	5,932	43,450	4,808	1.23	73
33	Kleenex	US	4,602	22,445	2,324	1.98	68
34	Wrigley's	US	4,404	8,809	2,005	2.20	69
35	AOL	US	4,329	23,979	2,600	1.66	52
36	Apple	US	4,283	5,574	5,941	0.72	59
37	Louis Vuitton	France	4,076	11,935	1,735	2.35	62
38	Barbie	US	3,792	8,196	1,913	1.98	70
39	Motorola	US	3,643	21,394	29,398	0.12	59
40	Adidas	Germany	3,596	**	4,616	0.78	67
41	Colgate	US	3,568	20,330	2,181	1.64	79
42	Hertz	US	3,527	4,691	4,238	0.83	69
43	IKEA	Sweden	3,464	**	6,244	0.55	56
44	Chanel	France	3,143	**	2,050	1.53	72
45	BP	UK	2,985	88,619	73,998	0.04	59
46	Bacardi	Cuba	2,895	**	1,901	1.52	71
47	Burger King	US	2,806	33,810	1,449	1.94	6
48	Moët & Chandon	France	2,804	11,935	1,339	2.09	70
49	Shell	UK	2,681	164,157	98,445	0.03	61
50	Rolex	Switzerland	2,423	**	1,409	1.72	64
51	Smirnoff	Russia	2,313	33,810	1,311	1.76	71
52	Heineken	Holland	2,184	14,886	2,031	1.08	74
53	Yahoo!	US	1,761	12,673	203	8.67	50
54	Ralph Lauren	US	1,648	2,479	1,471	1.12	53
55	Johnnie Walker	UK	1,634	33,810	969	1.69	69
56	Pampers	US	1,422	95,127	827	1.72	77
57	Amazon.com	US	1,361	18,510	610	2.23	57
58	Hilton	US	1,319	3,765	3,395	0.39	61
59	Guinness	Ireland	1,262	33,810	1,188	1.06	70
60	Marriott	US	1,193	2,278	7,729	0.15	55

** Information not available

Index